COVENANT

Making Commitments
That Count

David Otto

Abingdon Press
Nashville

Covenant: Making Commitments That Count

20/30: Bible Study for Young Adults

by David Otto

Copyright © 1999 by Abingdon Press

ISBN 0-687-08306-0

This book is printed on acid-free paper.

Manufactured in the United States of America.

00 01 02 03 04 05 06 07 08—10 9 8 7 6 5 4 3 2

CONTENTS

Meet the Writer 4

Welcome to *20/30* 5

How to Use This Resource 7

Organizing a Group 9

Sharing Leadership 11

Choosing Teaching Options 13

Using Break-Out Groups 15

Covenant: Making Commitments That Count 17

Session 1:
Covenants of Promise, Reward, and Responsibility 19

Session 2:
Intimacy as Covenant 27

Session 3:
Covenant With Creation 35

Session 4:
Living With Rules 43

Session 5:
Broken Promises 51

Session 6:
Making Sacrifices 59

Session 7:
Renewing Our Covenant With God 67

Case Studies 75

Service Learning Options 79

MEET THE WRITER

David Otto currently serves as Associate Professor of Religion at Centenary College in Shreveport, LA. Nationally recognized as a dynamic speaker and provocative scholar, David has published numerous works, including *Reality Check*, a guide to local churches in redesigning youth ministry for a new millennium. He can be seen regularly on the Odyssey Network on the long-running television series, *Scriptures Alive*, which explores social issues from biblical and theological perspectives.

WELCOME TO 20/30:
BIBLE STUDY FOR YOUNG ADULTS

The **20/30** Bible study series is offered for post-modern adults who want to participate in and help structure their own discoveries—in life, in relationships, in faith. In each of the volumes of this series, we will have the opportunity to use our own experience in life and faith to examine the biblical texts in new ways. We will examine biblical images that shape all of our lives, even if we are not immediately aware that they do.

Image Is Everything

Images are what shape our decisions. We may think or know certain important data that weigh heavily in a decision. We may value the advice and counsel of others. We may find that the stated or implied wishes of others influence what we do. But in the end, it is often the *image* we hold that makes the decision.

For example, perhaps you were deeply hurt by someone important to you— an employer, a friend, even a pastor. You know in your heart that the institution is not to blame or that friendships are based on more than one event. But the image shaped by the difficult experience is that the job, or the friend, or the church cannot be relied upon. You *know* better, but you just have to make a change anyway. The image was more powerful than the reason.

Images are powerful, and they are familiar. In each of the studies in this series, you will encounter a well-known image that will connect your familiar experiences with some basis in Scripture. You know what it's like to make agreements, to establish commitments, to give your word and expect to be trusted. *Covenant: Making Commitments That Count* engages you in study sessions that explain a variety of covenants, what happens when covenants are broken, how to have a faithful covenant to care for others and for the earth, and certainly, what it means to have this sacred covenant with God.

You know what it is like to move to a new place, to have to deal with transitions in school or work or in relationships. You have probably experienced changes in your family as you have grown up and moved out on your own. Some of these moves are gradual, just taken in stride. Others can be painful or abrupt; certainly life-changing. In *Exodus: Leaving Behind, Moving On*, you will appreciate learning how God is in the midst of those movements, no matter how minor or how transformational.

You know how important it is to have a sense of support and roots; to have friends and a life partner. *Community: Living Faithfully With Others* introduces you to Scriptures and life examples that delve into intimacy, work, family relationships, and more.

You have faith, but may also realize that it can mean many things. Is it belief or trust or waiting or moral behavior or something else? Or it is all those things? *Faith: Living a Spiritual Life* helps you examine your faith and grow as a Christian.

Experience, Faith, Growth, and Action

Each volume in this series will help you probe, on your own terms, how your experience links with your faith and how deepening your faith develops your life experience. If you need a prompt for your reflection, each volume has several pages of real life case studies. As your faith and commitment to Jesus Christ grow, you may be looking for ways to be involved in specific service opportunities. Several are listed on page 79.

We hope this series will help you encounter God through Scripture, reflection, and dialogue with others who desire to grow in faith, and to serve others. One image we hold is that God is in all things. God is certainly with you.

HOW TO USE THIS RESOURCE

Each session of this resource includes similar components or elements:
- a statement of the issue or question to be explored;
- several "voices" of persons who are currently dealing with that issue;
- exploration of biblical passages relative to the question raised;
- "Bible 101" boxes that provide insight about the study of the Bible;
- questions for reflection and discussion;
- suggested individual and group activities designed to bring the session to life;
- optional case studies (found in the back of the book);
- various service learning activities related to the session (found in the back of the book).

Choices, Choices, Choices

Collectively, these components mean one thing: *choice*. You have choices to make concerning how to use each session of this resource. Want just the nitty-gritty Bible reading, reflection, and study for personal or group use? Then focus your attention on just those components during your study time.

Like starting with real-life stories about issues then moving into how the Bible might be relevant? Start with the "voices" and move on from there. Use the "voices" to encourage group members to speak about their own experiences.

Prefer highly charged discussion encounters where many different viewpoints can be heard? Start the session with the biblical passages, followed by the questions and group activities. Be sure to compare the ideas found in the "Bible 101" boxes with your current ideas for more discussion. Want the major challenge of applying biblical principles to a difficult problem? After reading the biblical material, read one of the case studies, using the guidelines provided on page 14 or get involved with one of the service learning options, described on 79.

Great Versatility

This resource has been designed for many different uses. Some persons will use this resource for personal study and reflection. Others will want to explore the work with a small group of friends. And still other folks will see this book as a different type of Sunday school resource.

Spend some time thinking about your own questions, study habits, and learning styles or those of your small group. Then use the guidelines mentioned above to fashion each session into a unique Bible study session to meet those requirements.

Highly Participatory

As you will see, the Scriptures, "voices," commentary, and experience of group members will provide an opportunity for an active, engaging time together. The greatest challenge for a group leader might be "crowd control"—being sure everyone has the chance to put his or her ideas into the mix!

The Scriptures will help you and those who study with you to make connections between real-life issues and the Bible. This resource values and encourages personal participation as a means to fully understand and appreciate the intersection of personal belief with God's ongoing work in each and every life.

ON ORGANIZING A SMALL GROUP

Learning with a small group of persons offers certain advantages over studying by yourself. First, you will hopefully encounter different opinions and ideas, making the experience of Bible study a richer and more challenging event. Second, any leadership responsibilities can be shared among group members. Third, different persons will bring different talents. Some will be deep thinkers while other group members will be creative giants. Some persons will be newcomers to the Bible; their questions and comments will help others clarify their deeply held assumptions.

So how does one go about forming a small group? Follow the steps below and see how easy this task can be.

- **Read through the resource carefully.** Think about the ideas presented, the questions raised, and the exercises suggested. If the sessions of this work excite you, it will be easier for you to share your enthusiasm to others.

- **Spend some time thinking about church members, friends, and co-workers who might find the sessions of this resource interesting**. On a sheet of paper, write down two characteristics or talents you see in each person that would make them an attractive Bible study group member. Some talents might include "deep thinker," "creative wizard," or "committed Christian." Remember: the best small group has members who differ in learning styles, talents, ideas, and convictions, but who respect the dignity and integrity of the other members.

- **Most functional small groups have 7-15 members.** Make a list of potential group members that doubles your target number. For instance, if you would like a small group of seven to ten members, be prepared to invite fourteen to twenty persons.

- **Once your list of potential candidates is complete, decide on a tentative location and time.** Of course, the details can be negotiated with those persons who accept the invitation, but you need to sound definitive and clear to prospective group members. "We will initially set Wednesday night from 7-9 P.M. at my house for our meeting time" will sound more attractive than "Well, I don't know either when or where we would be meeting, but I hope you will consider joining us."

- **Make initial contact with perspective group members short, sweet, and to the point.** Say something like, "We are putting together a Bible study using a different kind of resource. When would be a good time to show you the resource and talk about the study?" Establishing a special time to make the invitation takes the pressure off the perspective group member to make a quick decision.

- **Show up at the decided time and place.** Talk with each perspective member individually. Bring a copy of the resource with you. Show them what excites you about the study and mention the two unique characteristics or talents you feel they would offer the group. Tell them the initial meeting time and location and how many weeks the small group will meet. Also mention that the need for a new time or location could be discussed during the first group meeting. Ask for a commitment to come to the first session. Thank them for their time.

- **Give a quick phone call or email to thank all persons for their consideration and interest.** Remind persons of the time and location of the first meeting.

- **Be organized.** Use the first group meeting to get acquainted. Briefly describe the seven sessions. Have a book for each group member and discuss sharing responsibilities for leadership.

LEADING AND SHARING LEADERSHIP

So the responsibility to lead the group has fallen on you? Don't sweat it. Follow these simple suggestions and you will razzle and dazzle the group with your expertise.

■ **Read the session carefully.** Look up all the Bible passages. Take careful notes about the ideas, statements, questions, and activities in the session. Try all the activities.

■ **Using 20-25 blank index cards, write one idea, activity, Bible passage, or question from the session on each card** until you either run out of material or cards. Be sure to look at the case studies and service learning options. Number the cards so they will follow the order of the session.

■ **Spend a few moments thinking about the members of your group.** How many like to think about ideas, concepts, or problems? How many need to "feel into" an idea by storytelling, worship, prayer, or group activities? Who are the "actors" who prefer a hands-on or participatory approach, such as an art project or simulation, to grasp an idea? Write down the names of all group members and record whether you believe them to be a THINKER, FEELER, or an ACTOR.

■ **Place all the index cards in front of you in the order in which they originally appeared in the session.** Looking at that order, ask yourself: (1) Where is the "Head" of the session—the key ideas or concepts? (2) Where is the "Heart" of the session in which persons will have a deep feeling response? (3) Where are the "Feet"—those activities that ask the group to put the ideas and feelings to use? Separate the cards into three stacks: HEAD, HEART, and FEET.

■ **Now construct the "body" for your class.** Shift the cards around, using a balance of HEAD, HEART, and FEET cards to determine which activities you will do and in what order. This will be your group's unique lesson plan. Try to choose as many cards as you have group members. Then, match the cards: HEAD and THINKERS; HEART and FEELERS; FEET and ACTORS for each member of the group. Don't forget a card for yourself. For instance, if your group has ten members, you should have about ten cards.

■ **Develop the leadership plan.** Invite group members prior to the session to assist in the leadership. Show them the unique lesson plan you developed. Ask for their assistance in developing and/or leading each segment of the session as well an introduction and a closing ritual or worship experience.

Your lesson plan should start with welcoming the participants. Hopefully everyone will have read the session ahead of time. Then, begin to move through the activity cards in the order of your unique session plan, sharing the leadership as you have agreed.

You may have chosen to have all the HEAD cards together, followed by the HEART cards. This would introduce the session's content, followed by helping group members "feel into" the issue through interactive stories, questions, and exercises with all group members. Feel free to add more storytelling, discussion, prayer, mediation, or worship.

You may have chosen to use the FEET cards to end the session. Ask the group, "What difference should this session make in our daily lives?" You or the ACTORS should introduce the FEET cards as possible ways to discern a response. Ensuring that group members leave with a few practical suggestions for doing something different during the week is the point of this section of the unique lesson plan.

■ **Remember: leading the group does not mean "Do it all yourself."** With a little planning, you can enlist the talents of many group members. By inviting group members to lead parts of the session that feel comfortable for them, you will model and encourage shared leadership. Welcome their interests in music, prayer, worship, Bible, and so on, to develop innovative and creative Bible study sessions that can transform lives in the name of Jesus Christ.

CHOOSING TEACHING OPTIONS

This young adult series was designed, written, and produced out of an understanding of the attributes, concerns, joys, and faith issues of young adults. With great care and integrity, this image-based print resource was developed to connect biblical events and relationships with contemporary, real-life situations of young adults. Its pages will promote Christian relationships and community, support new biblical learning, encourage spiritual development, and empower faithful decision-making and action.

This study is well-suited to young adults and may be used confidently and effectively. But with the great diversity within the young adult population, not every line of this study will be written "just for you." To be most relevant, some portions of the study material need to be tailored to fit your particular group. Adjustments for a good fit involve making choices from options offered by the resource. This customizing may be done easily by a designated leader who is familiar with the layout of the resource and the young adults who are using it.

What to Expect

In this study, Scripture and real-life images mesh together to provoke a personal response. Young adults will find themselves thinking, feeling, imagining, questioning, making decisions, professing faith, building connections, inviting discipleship, taking action, and making a difference. Scripture is at the core of each session. Scenarios weave in the dimensions of real-life. Narrative and text boxes frame plenty of teaching options to offer young adults.

Each session is part of a cohesive volume, but is designed to stand alone. One session is not dependent on knowledge or experience accumulated from other sessions. A group leader can freely choose from the teaching options in an individual session without wondering about how it might affect the other sessions.

A Good Fit

For a better fit, alter the session based on what is known about the young adult participants. Young adults are a diverse constituency with varied experiences, interests, needs, and values. There is really no single defining characteristic that links young adults. Specific information about the age, employment status, household, personal relationships, and lifestyle among participants will equip a leader to make choices that ensure a good fit.

- **Customize.** Read through the session. Notice how scenarios and teaching options move from integrating Scripture and real-life dimensions to inviting a response.

- **Look at the scenario(s).** How real is the presentation of real-life? Say that the main character is a professional, white male, married, in his late 20's and caught in a workplace dilemma that entangles his immediate superior and a subordinate from his division. Perhaps your group members are mostly college students and recent graduates, unmarried, and still on the way to being "settled." There are many differences between the man in the scenario and the group members using this resource.

  As a leader, you could choose to eliminate the case study, substitute it with another scenario (there are several more choices on pages 75–78), claim the validity of the dilemma, and shift the spotlight from the main character to the subordinate, or modify the description of the main character. Break-Out groups based on age or employment experience might also be used to accommodate the differences and offer a better fit.

- **Look at the teaching options.** How are the activities propelling participants toward a personal response? Perhaps the Scripture study requires more meditative quiet than is possible and a more academic, verbal, or artistic approach would offer a better fit. Maybe more direct decisions or actions would fit better than more passive or logical means. Try to keep a balance, though, that allows participants to "get out of their head" to reflect and also to move toward action.

  Conceivably, there could just be too much in any one session. As a leader, you can pick and choose among teaching options, substitute case studies, take two meetings to do one session, and adapt any process to make a better fit. The tailoring process can be evaluated as adjustments are made. Judge the fit every time you meet. Ask questions that gauge relevance and assess how the resource has stretched minds, encouraged discipleship, and changed lives.

USING BREAK-OUT GROUPS

20/30 Break-Out groups are small groups that encourage the personal sharing of lives and the gospel. The name "Break-Out" is a sweeping term that includes a variety of small group settings. A Break-Out group may resemble a Bible study group, an interest group, a sharing group, or other types of Christian fellowship groups.

Break-Out groups offer young adults a chance to belong and personally relate to one another. Members are known, nurtured, and heard by others. Young adults may agree and disagree while maximizing the exchange of ideas, information, or options. They might explore, confront, and resolve personal issues and feelings with empathy and support. Participants can challenge and hold each other accountable to a personalized faith and stretch its links to real-life and service.

Forming Break-Out Groups

The nature of these small Break-Out groups will depend on the context and design of the specific session. On occasion the total group of participants will be divided for a particular activity. Break-Out groups will differ from one session to the next. Variations may involve the size of the group, how group members are divided, or the task of the group. Break-Out groups may also be used to accommodate differences and help tailor the session plan for a better fit. In some sessions, specific group assembly instructions will be provided. For other sessions, decisions regarding the size or division of small groups will be made by the designated leader. Break-Out groups may be in the form of pairs or trios, family-sized groups of 3-6 members, or groups of up to ten members.

They may be arranged simply by grouping persons seated next to each other or in more intentional ways by common interests, characteristics, or life experience. Consider creating Break-Out groups according to age; gender; type of household, living arrangements, or love relationships; vocation, occupation, career, or employment status; common or built-in connections; lifestyle; values or perspective; or personal interests or traits.

Membership

The membership of Break-Out groups will vary from session to session, or even within specific sessions. Young adults need to work at knowing and being known, so that there can be a balance between Break-Out groups that are more similar and those that reflect greater diversity. There may be times when more honest communication, trust, or accountability may be desired and group leaders will need to be free to self-select small group members.

It is important for *20/30* Break-Out groups to practice acceptance and to value the worth of others. The potential for small groups to encourage personal sharing and significant relationships is enhanced when members agree to exercise active listening skills, keep confidences, expect authenticity, foster trust, and develop ways of loving one another. All group members contribute to the development and function of Break-Out groups. Designated leaders especially need to model manners of hospitality and help ensure that each group member is respected.

Invitational Listening

Consider establishing an "invitational listening" routine that validates the perspective and affirms the voice of each group member. After a question or statement is posed, pause and allow time to think—not everyone thinks on their feet or talks out loud to think. Then, initiate conversation by inviting one group member, by name, to talk. This person may either choose to talk or to "pass." Either way, this person is honored and is offered an opportunity to speak and be heard. This person carries on the ritual by inviting another group member, by name, to speak. The process continues until all have been invited, by name, to talk. As each one invites another, the responsibility of acceptance and hospitality in the Break-Out groups is shared among all its members.

Study group members Break-Out to belong, to share the gospel, to care, and to watch over one another in Christian love. "So deeply do we care for you that we are determined to share with you not only the gospel of God but also our own selves, because you have become very dear to us" (1 Thessalonians 2:8).

COVENANT:
MAKING COMMITMENTS
THAT COUNT

Relationships define who we are. Some of us are "employees," indicating a commitment to a place of employment, to certain tasks and results, to coworkers to be dependable members of a working team. Others of us are "students," suggesting a relationship with a school, college, classroom, teachers, books, and other students. Others are called "Christians," implying a series of relationships to God, Jesus Christ, history, denominations, Bible, rituals, and daily practices. Many persons might be called "brother," "sister," "mother," or "father," denoting a particular type of relationship with a select group of persons. Even our names were given to us to suggest a specific connection to a group of persons: our parents, ancestors, and culture. And many persons want to experience God's love and guidance within all of these relationships.

Understanding Covenants

In this volume, we will explore the biblical idea of *covenant*, a term Christians often use when the Spirit of God is a present and active member of a relationship. Many of us want covenant marriages, friendships, or business partnerships, suggesting that God should play an important and ongoing role in the way we work, play, study, live, and love with others. But keeping focused on God as an ever-present partner in all our relationships can become quite an undertaking, especially when daily pressures demand so much of our attention.

This resource for young adults hopes to connect and confront our contemporary questions about relationships with key ideas, images, and insights from Scripture. Designed as a unique Bible study approach, each session identifies specific issues about covenant, looks at biblical ideas that explore these issues, and suggests helpful ways to make covenant relationships more joyful and fulfilling.

An Orientation to the Sessions

In Session One, we will learn about three types of biblical covenants present in our daily lives. Biblical ideas that can challenge and shape our intimate relationships make Session Two special. Our relationship with the earth as stewards is explored in the third session; while the job of living with rules at home, church, and the workplace becomes the task of Session Four. The pain, heartache, and possibilities of broken relationships find words of scriptural comfort and direction in Session Five. The next-to-last session looks at sacrifice in new and meaningful ways for today's world, and Session Seven declares the necessity of renewing our relationship with God and others by turning to the Bible for models and advice.

A Unique Study

So what makes this study so different? First, it focuses on the events of your life. In each session you will be encouraged to link key biblical ideas to situations you probably deal with on a regular basis. Real-life issues are represented within each session, using everyday language.

Second, each session incorporates new ideas and insights from modern biblical scholarship, without all the fancy words. You will be introduced to the idea that many books of the Old and New Testament reflect the work of many different writers. Concepts from the time and life of these authors that may have assisted them in giving shape to God's inspired message will be mentioned. Special "Bible 101" boxes will indicate more advanced ideas that may challenge your current assumptions of the Bible. If you like that type of encounter, use them. If not, just skip them and move on. You get to choose.

Third, you are asked to draw your own conclusions. Some Bible studies seek to give you the "right" answer. In this book, you will be presented a basic question, provided several different responses and asked to make up your own mind. Your own experience is valid; it is at least a beginning place for added insight and growth.

Fourth, this resource is flexible. Want to study on your own? Fine. Grab it and get started. Want to pull together some friends and work as a small group? Sounds great. Need something a little different for your Sunday school class? Look no further.

Finally, this resource makes the assumption that the Bible is deeply relevant to the 21st-century world. If there was ever a time the world could use a little divine guidance, it's now. Maybe this different kind of study will spark new interest in a timeless, sacred work. Or at least suggest that God still has something to say to the post-modern world. May this work nurture renewal and growth in your relationship with God through Jesus Christ. Peace.

COVENANTS OF PROMISE, REWARD, & RESPONSIBILITY

This session will explore three biblical models of covenant and their relationship to our daily lives.

GETTING STARTED

"The word *covenant* sounds like something old and biblical. I cannot imagine the word having much meaning for Christians today." Melissa, age 25

"Other than my marriage—and maybe my home mortgage—a covenant is really not a practical term." Philip, age 31

"The Bible speaks of a covenant God made with Moses, but Christians were excused from all those laws with the death of Jesus ... right?" Arney, age 22

Getting Started
Ask group members to rate the three statements of Melissa, Philip, and Arney, using this scale: 1) I fully agree, 2) I somewhat agree, 3) I neither agree nor disagree, 4) I somewhat disagree, and 5) I totally disagree with the statement. Encourage group members to explain their responses.

What Is a Covenant?
Write a brief description of a covenant and then compare descriptions.

Respond to these playful (and provocative) analogies:
1. A covenant is like a bathtub because . . .
2. Keeping promises is like dancing because . . .
3. Rewards are like eating dessert because . . .
4. Following rules is like the first day on the job because . . .

SO, WHAT IS A COVENANT?

In simple terms, a covenant is a dynamic give-and-take agreement between two parties. We know of many covenants in our lives: vows exchanged in friendship and marriage, agreements struck with banks or other loaning institutions, credit card usage, or even a handshake. But are all covenants alike? Is a handshake, for example, just as serious as a promise to repay thousands of dollars?

When we turn to the Bible for assistance, we find three basic covenant types described. By looking carefully at these three biblical models of covenant, we can understand something about the various

types of covenants in our lives today. We will also ask the question: How seriously should we take those covenants from the Old and New Testaments?

A PROMISE IS A PROMISE: PROMISSORY COVENANTS

A Promise Is a Promise
So what promissory covenants have you entered recently?

Form two teams. In three minutes each team should write as many examples of promissory covenants as possible. Remember: promissory covenants involve a quick exchange between two parties with no further obligations.

The first type of biblical covenant can be found throughout both Testaments. Commonly known as a *promissory covenant*, this dynamic agreement describes a rapid, momentary exchange between two parties. Both parties give or promise something to the other party and then they go their separate ways. A simple business transaction.

Read Genesis 21:22-34. What a great example of a promissory covenant! In this narrative, Abraham, one of the major names you may remember from the Old Testament, enters into an on-the-spot agreement with King Abimelech, who "accidentally" took Abraham's wife, Sarah, as his own. Actually, Abraham told Abimelech that Sarah was Abraham's sister. (For the whole story, read Genesis 20:1-18.)

In Genesis 21:22-24, 27, 31, King Abimelech is rather leery of conducting business with Abraham, given that Lord God blamed Abimelech for taking Sarah as a wife. So the king asks Abraham to swear by God that he has dealt honestly with both Abimelech and his children. Abraham swears by the name of God. And that is all there is to a promissory covenant.

In a second version of the story (Genesis 21:25-26, 28-30), Abraham complains to King Abimelech about a well that Abimelech's servants confiscated from Abraham. With a quick exchange of property (the ancient equivalent to money) a deal of ownership is struck. The end. No more business.

Read Genesis 21:22-34, which provides two great examples: a "handshake" and an exchange of "money." The team that names the most uncontested examples wins. As a sign of good faith, members of the winning team should shake the hands of the other team members.

What rules or conditions should direct our daily use of promissory covenants? Why?

Should Christians engage in such rituals in the same way as non-Christians? Explain.

REWARD-BASED COVENANTS

Reward-Based Covenants

Read Genesis 12:1-9.

Provide paper; have it divided into four squares of equal size. Label each box with one of the following terms: "Offspring," "Land," "Blessings," and "Protection." Allow a few minutes for persons to write in the appropriate square answers to the questions below.

What does it mean for you to be connected to Lord God through the rewards of offspring (the reward of your own birth and the responsibility of bringing life into being), land (managing the resources of the earth and living as the Earth's beneficiary), blessings (the specific joys of your life), and protection (ways in which God looks after you)?

What does it mean to name these items as rewards in your life today?

Discuss these personal responses. Then pray together, giving thanks for the specific rewards listed by group members.

Genesis 12:1-9 provides a superb example of a Reward-Based (or Royal Grant) covenant. In this second type of biblical covenant, one party gives a reward to the other party, who promises to be faithful and true to the one providing the reward or incentive. Lord God promises Abraham, then called Abram, many offspring, a piece of land, numerous blessings, and divine protection. And what did Abraham promise in return? Not a single thing. Instead, Abraham responds to Lord God with love, loyalty, and locomotion: Abraham goes wherever Lord God tells him.

Read Genesis 12:1-9 carefully. Identify the specific rewards offered Abraham. Notice Abraham is not required to promise Lord God anything in return. Like the promissory covenant, the Reward-Based model can be found throughout the Old and New Testaments.

The Abrahamic Covenant (the formal name for Genesis 12:1-9) is considered one of the three most sacred covenants in the Old Testament. Since Lord God's promise passed from one generation to the next, it is commonly believed that all descendants of Abraham inherited this covenant. Tradition suggests that all persons of Jewish, Islamic, and Christian descent are bound to Lord God by this set of promises.

Read Genesis 15:1-6. Notice that Lord God restates the rewards. Notice Abraham, in a straightforward manner, reminds Lord God of a particular reward: offspring. In the biblical tradition of Reward-Based covenants, it is acceptable protocol to remind God of promises made.

The manner in which Abraham reminds Lord God of the promise for offspring appears strange: "O Lord GOD, what will you give me, for I continue childless, and the heir of my house is Eliezer of Damascus?" (Genesis 15:2).

An ancient Canaanite custom, known as *Nuzi Law*, states that should a man of property die without a male heir, all of his property (including his wife) will be inherited by his chief servant. Apparently Abraham thought he would die before Lord God kept the promise concerning offspring. In a calm and loving manner, Lord God reminds Abraham he will have children—more than Abraham can count.

DISCUSS
What does it mean for Christians to share this sacred promise of Abraham with Jews and Muslims? In what specific ways can we show God love, loyalty, and locomotion?

Read Genesis 15:1-6. BIBLE

In Genesis 15:2-3, Abraham appears to question Lord God's willingness to keep a divine promise. Under what conditions should we be willing to call God's actions into question?

After Lord God and Abraham look at the stars together, we are told Abraham "believed the LORD. . . ." Does this mean that before looking at the stars with the Lord, Abraham did not believe God? Have there ever been times in your life when you found it hard to believe God? Explain.

". . . and the LORD reckoned it to him [Abraham] as righteousness" (Genesis 15:6). The term *righteousness* in Hebrew (the original language of most of the Old Testament) refers to a set of balanced scales. How is the deal between Abraham and Lord God now "balanced?" What actions could tip the scales out of balance?

Covenants of Promise, Reward, and Responsibility

RULE-BASED COVENANTS

Rule-Based Covenants

Unscramble the following words to discover examples of communities that operate under Rule-Based covenants. Spend a few moments discussing how each community functions under this covenant type.
1) SRIOPN
2) IIENRSTUYV
3) LAMIYF
4) TICY
5) TEYNOPMMEL

Humans live by rules. When growing up, we lived by the rules of our parents, schools, and communities. As young adults, we live by the rules of society, church, and perhaps an employer. In all cases, we follow the rules in return for safety, order, and status.

In Rule-Based (or Suzerainty) covenants, found within both the Old and New Testaments, a powerful force (usually God or a foreign nation) imposes rules and regulations on a set of people (usually Israel or Judah), who promise to follow these laws and ordinances in return for protection and support. Disobedience of rules could, and often did, mean bad consequences for either the violator or for his or her community.

Biblical Studies 101: Terms to Know

Pentateuch comes from a Greek word meaning "five books." The term is often used by Christians to describe Genesis, Exodus, Leviticus, Numbers, and Deuteronomy as a single collection.

Torah comes from ancient Hebrew. While commonly translated as "law," this term suggests a larger concept: the words of God for the people of God who must listen. Torah is used primarily within Jewish communities to describe Genesis, Exodus, Leviticus, Numbers, and Deuteronomy as a single collection.

Mosaic Covenant refers to the hundreds of specific obligations recorded within Torah. Until recent times, most persons assumed Moses wrote the Pentateuch while on Mount Sinai. As a result, this collection of obligations (often called "the Law" in the New Testament) became associated directly with this famous man of faith.

Whose rules are the most important for you? Why? What place does your own experience (or lack of experience) have in establishing authority and rule-based covenants?

Write out your own set of Ten Commandments in their order of importance to you. Be prepared to explain your choices.

Jewish and Christian traditions consider the first five books of the Old Testament an example of this covenant. Known as *Torah* or *Pentateuch*, these writings contain over 613 laws that God's people have followed for generations. Many religious communities still follow these rules and regulations today.

More than just the Ten Commandments (Exodus 20:1-17; Deuteronomy 5:6-21), the *Mosaic Covenant* describes the specific behaviors and practices required of God's people, regulating everything from food customs to sexual practices. Want to explore these laws? You may spend a few moments browsing these collections:

- Book of the Covenant: civil and religious laws (Exodus 20:22-23:33)
- The Ritual Decalogue: Ten Commandments (Exodus 34:10-26)
- Instructions to Ancient Religious Leaders (Exodus 25-31)
- Laws of the Ancient Priests (Leviticus 1-18)
- Purification Laws (Leviticus 19–26)

So, should Christians keep the obligations of Mosaic covenant? The short form is: strive to live your life lovingly and in accordance with God's will. The rest of the answer depends on your reading of the Bible and the Christian community to which you belong. For instance, Matthew 5:17-20 suggests that Jesus required his followers to keep every letter of the law (Mosaic Covenant) while Mark 12:28-31 implies Jesus thought only one commandment should be followed: love God with all you have and your neighbor as yourself.

Some Christian communities assume the death and resurrection of Jesus frees us

Closer Look

LOOK CLOSER

Imagine that your group is made up of at least one diplomat, archeologist/historian, theologian, sociologist, economist, lawyer, and others of your choosing. You are about to enter negotiations with another country to establish a mutually satisfactory living and working relationship.

Read these collections of covenantal laws, from the Book of the Covenant through the Purification Law, which are or have been the basis of your society.

Which of these covenants are still binding for your society? Which form the core of values? seem antiquated now? must be shared (or insisted upon) with this other nation?

BIBLE

Should Christians keep the Mosaic covenant? Read **Matthew 7:17-20** and **Mark 12:28-31** and debate the question.

from the obligations of Mosaic covenant, while other denominations believe the most Christ-like life one could lead adheres to the Law of Moses. Some Christians will grant validity to one obligation in Torah while ignoring others. To find out what your denomination believes, ask a pastor or become familiar with the doctrine of your tradition.

LAST WORDS

The Old and New Testaments contain many covenants between humans and God. These dynamic relationships can be defined using three categories: Promissory, Reward-Based, and Rule-Based. The Bible shows how God called persons into special relationships of promise, reward, and responsibility. And through Jesus Christ, God still calls us into these sacred covenants. As a people of the Promise, we are asked to behave in ways that mirror God's intention for our lives. As a community of believers, we inherit the rewards of faith given by God to our ancestors. As followers of Jesus Christ, we are called to be responsible to the obligations made explicit through the Bible, our religious traditions, and society.

CLOSING PRAYER

God, our ancestors entered into covenants with you many years ago. Today we gather to give thanks for these historic relationships. But we also gather in anticipation of hearing your voice call us. May we be receptive to your presence, God, as you speak to us. Amen.

CASE STUDY

Last Words

Compare the three types of biblical covenants with the comments of Melissa, Philip, and Arney on page 19. What meaning does *covenant* have for you now?

DISCUSS

Think about your own covenants. Which two or three are the most important for you? Why? Is a covenantal relationship with God and Jesus Christ in your top three? Have you ever felt invited into such a relationship with Christ? If so, what was that experience like?

CLOSE

Closing Prayer

If you feel that God is calling you to join in a covenant, take time now to make or renew that commitment. Then close with the prayer.

INTIMACY AS COVENANT

> This session will examine the nature of intimacy by exploring key passages of Scripture. **Please note:** Conversations about intimacy can become difficult for some persons, especially in a public place like a study group. This session will suggest topics and questions of a personal nature you may either explore during the session or in a more private setting with others.

"My relationship with Marge is so great; I have never felt more alive."

"Victoria and I have been dating for several months. Recently, things have become quite serious. I wonder: Am I really ready for a commitment?"

"Leslie and I are such good friends. At times we seem to read each other's minds. Even if I get married, I know we will always be there for one another."

"Relationships stink. I've given up on intimacy. It's just me and my pets from this day forward."

What is intimacy? In what way does intimacy suggest a covenant? How can the Bible assist in love and covenant? In this session we will explore issues of intimacy between close friends and partners.

Getting Started
Ask group members to form pairs and choose the opening comment that best summarizes their own understanding of intimacy. Ask each person to comment briefly on his or her choice.

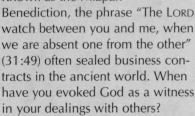

As God Is My Witness . . .
Read Genesis 31:43-49. Known as the Mizpah Benediction, the phrase "The LORD watch between you and me, when we are absent one from the other" (31:49) often sealed business contracts in the ancient world. When have you evoked God as a witness in your dealings with others?

Under what conditions would you evoke God as a witness to an intimate relationship? Find a copy of your denomination's service for marriage. How many times does God get called into action? Most Protestant traditions consider both the pastor and God as witnesses to marriage, an agreement enacted by the man and woman.

Speaking of Love
Read 1 Corinthians 13, known by many modern Christians as the "Love Chapter." According to this ancient poem, what is love? On a large sheet of paper, write down the key attributes of love found in this text. On a scale between 1 through 10 (1 meaning "Never" and 10 meaning "Always") spend a few moments rating yourself on how well your behaviors with loved ones parallel these characteristics. Share your rating with another member of the group. Discuss what specific behaviors could raise your "Love Ratings."

AS GOD IS MY WITNESS. . .

Throughout the Old and New Testaments, persons made covenants with other persons. Jonathan entered a covenant with David (1 Samuel 18:1-5; 23:15-18), Ruth pledged her life to Naomi (Ruth 1:1-18), Jesus forged a new relationship with his disciples at a meal (Mark 14:22-25) and a man and woman entered the special relationship of sexual intimacy (Song of Solomon 8:5-14). What do these references to covenant have in common?

First, *covenants between persons in the Bible usually evoke Lord God as a witness to the contract*. Through both poetic language and blunt pronouncements, one person requests God to oversee the agreement established. Sometimes the agreement is an issue of business, like one struck between Jacob and Laban (Genesis 31:43-44). On other occasions, God is called to witness the deep love and commitment between two persons, like the man and woman in Song of Solomon, or David and Jonathan in the Samuel narratives.

SPEAKING OF LOVE...

Second, *covenants between persons use the language of love and intimacy*. More than just mushy words, terms of love and intimacy suggest the desire of one person to be completely and honestly known by another human being. Of course, one can be known in a variety of ways: physical, sexual, mental, spiritual, and social. Deciding how we are to be known by others is a key ingredient to fashioning a Christian lifestyle of intimacy and love.

For instance, ask a group member to read aloud Ruth's words to her mother-in-law, Naomi (Ruth 1:16-17). Identify the words and phrases that suggest intimacy and love. Think about a modern day paraphrase of these words. What would such a statement sound like? To whom would you be willing to make such a statement?

After reading the "Biblical Studies 101" box, read Ruth 3. Does that story mean what I think it means? As a group, discuss the actions of Naomi, Ruth, and Boaz. What types of intimacy are described in this story? Why would such a story be included in the Bible? What role does God play in this chapter?

What, for you, are the acceptable behaviors that must be negotiated to establish mutuality and respect? How would you define physical intimacy? sexual intimacy? In what ways might these two types of intimacy be different?

Biblical Studies 101: "Getting to 'Know' You"

Did you know that both the Old and New Testaments are full of euphemisms, nice terms for describing rather uncomfortable situations or topics? For instance, in the Old Testament, for a man and woman to "know" each other can mean for them to have sexual intercourse. The term "feet" is often used as a euphemism for male genitalia. When Paul says "fallen asleep" (I Thessalonians 4:13), he is saying that somebody has died.

Often the writers of the Old and New Testament spoke euphemistically about issues of intimacy, love, and death. With this new knowledge, the story of Ruth and Boaz on the threshing floor (Ruth 3) takes on a new meaning for the reader while raising significant questions concerning intimacy, sex, and covenant.

Some persons may find it odd for persons of the same gender to make such declarations of love and intimacy to one another. But if intimacy refers to becoming fully known by another human being, then honest and open relationships—regardless of gender—seem appropriate. It should be stated, however, mutuality and respect for the other person demands a careful negotiation of acceptable behaviors. A common definition of intimacy must exist between persons for true love to emerge.

Consider the variety of same-sex covenants. **Read 1 Samuel 18:1-5; 23:15-18; Ruth 1:1-18; Mark 14:22-25.** What types of intimacy do you think is important within these relationships?

R-E-S-P-E-C-T: FIND OUT WHAT IT MEANS TO ME

SMALL GROUP

R-E-S-P-E-C-T
Have group members read aloud the Scripture passages mentioned in this section. After each passage is read, have the group decide on a definition of "family" and "respect." Write this definition on a large sheet of paper all group members can see.

So Christian covenants of intimacy possess a third characteristic: *They must promote extreme respect for the other party.* For instance, read Genesis 2:24: "Therefore a man leaves his father and his mother and clings to his wife, and they become one flesh." The term "one flesh" reflects an ancient understanding of mutuality we could call "family-ing"; that is, considering the other person as a blood relative whose life and body are as important as your own. This intimacy tradition of "family-ing" occurs frequently in the New Testament (John 19:26-27; Mark 3:31-35; Colossians 3:12-15), suggesting God has historically expected humans to enter into bonds of sacred respect and mutuality with one another.

In healthy relationships, each individual is respected, loved, and treasured for their unique gifts and qualities. But two persons, fashioned as a couple, forge an additional identity, one measured on the grounds of mutuality and respect for the other. Consider our friends Kristen and Keifer. How well do they function as a couple, given our definition of intimacy?

Kristen: Keifer and I have been dating for over a year, and I really love him. But my friends think he's not as supportive of me as he could be. While he spends a lot of time at work and with friends, I still think he makes as much time for me as possible. But my friends think I deserve somebody who will place me as a higher priority.

Keifer: Kristen is great fun. OK, so she's a little silly and illogical at times, but it's that playful quality that I really like. I do think she resents me at times, but these moments pass quickly. I let her do anything she wants and tell her when I will be working late or going out with my buddies. Personally, I think the openness of the relationship helps us last as a couple.

DISCUSS

How can we show respect for the personhood of those persons whom we cherish? for their bodies? for their dreams and desires? How does a healthy image of self set the stage for mutuality?

CASE STUDY

Ask the men of the group to read Kristen's comments and the women to read those of Kiefer. Discuss these questions: What issues do Kristen and Kiefer raise? How do these persons understand each other? their own expectations? their expectations of their partner? intimacy? What advice, if any, would you offer these friends? Does the Bible add any power to your advice?

OR, if you prefer, put a case of your own on the table (anonymously or not) in which expectations and/or values seem to be at variance and ask the same cluster of questions.

IT'S ALL ABOUT YOU: NOT

Fourth, *intimacy calls us to place the life of the other party on the same level as our own.* This action requires a great deal of communication between persons. It would be difficult for a friend, spouse, or loved one to demonstrate intimacy unless both persons promised to share the details of their life with the other. Sometimes intimate relationships dissolve because communication on this deep level ceases. Sharing of our-

SMALL

GROUP

It's All About You: NOT
Move back into groups of two. Describe to one another a time when you found it difficult to risk within a relationship. How did you resolve this situation?

In your "intimate" group of two, respond to the following situations in terms of how you might feel, what you might do, and what biblical witness comes to mind that helps you.

- Your partner or friend keeps breaking promises.
- Your partner or friend has physical desires for you. You do not hold the same desires for him or her.
- You have physical desires for a dear friend who is involved currently with somebody else.
- You suspect emotional or physical unfaithfulness on the part of your partner.
- You feel distant from your friend or partner but fear if you say something about your feelings it will be experienced as rejection.

Closer Look
If you have not done so already, spend a few moments reading the short book of Ruth. Perhaps you can find a film adaptation of the story at a local video store (but read the book before seeing the movie). You could even surf the Web, looking for adaptations, interpretations, and ideas concerning the main characters. What key words could you search for to narrow your focus, given the focus of this session?

selves calls for a level of risk-taking that can feel threatening, especially if our own history of relationships stinks. Some of us come from families in which our parents fought, bickered, or divorced. Many of us have experienced the pain of betrayal when somebody we loved and trusted hurt us with their words and actions. But these past encounters do not mean we are destined for a life of emptiness or superficial relationships. We must go through the tough but productive process of healing so we can let other persons into our lives and give love another chance.

MENDING BROKEN HEARTS, BIBLICAL STYLE

Let's go back to the story of Ruth and Naomi. Notice Ruth's proclamation of love and intimacy (1:16-17) is followed with the statement, "When Naomi saw that she was determined to go with her, she said no more to her." So much for mutuality! Remember, Naomi's husband and two sons had died unexpectedly. Without the protection of a male relative, her survival was at stake. She even felt Lord God had turned from her. Her track record on positive relationships seemed pretty bad.

But Ruth, as a partner-in-intimacy, stayed by her side. Through patient loving and honest sharing, Naomi began to love Ruth. By 3:1-5, Naomi provides Ruth with advice on how to enter a new level of intimacy with Boaz. Only through the healing love of Ruth could Naomi resurrect the positive, life affirming ideas of intimacy from her past and render helpful advice to Ruth. By the story's end, Naomi is breast-feeding Ruth and Boaz's first child and has once again felt the love of God and family.

So how did the transformation of Naomi occur? First, Ruth provided constancy in her relationship with Naomi: she kept her promises and behaved in a life-affirming manner. Second, Ruth made sincere statements of love and affection to Naomi, even when Naomi found it difficult to reciprocate. Third, Ruth supported Naomi through the tough times. Fourth, without ignoring or discounting Naomi's losses, Ruth encouraged Naomi to realize that relational disappointments or setbacks in the past need not determine her present behavior; intimacy requires acting on possibilities. Finally, Ruth helped Naomi realize that God had never forsaken her and always stood ready to embrace her within the arms of sacred community and prayer.

Using the story of Ruth and Naomi as a guideline to measuring sacred covenants between persons, what advice could we offer our friends Julita, Carlos, Ben, Timothy, and Chris?

Julita: When Carlos and I separated for two months, I went out one time with Miguel. Now Carlos thinks I am and always will be unfaithful. We had time apart because I grew tired of seeing him check out every single person he met. I guess this is the end for good.

Mending Hearts, Biblical Style
CASE STUDY Using whatever you glean from Ruth to evaluate the situations of our friends Julita, Carlos, Ben, Timothy, and Chris, respond to the following questions and statements:

- What, in your opinion, are the positive and negative values of each character?
- Tell a story about each character's possible past relationships. How can our past shape our present?
- Which character comes closest to mentioning some of your own issues with intimacy?
- What strength, direction, or words of assurance does your Christian faith offer you during your struggle for authentic intimacy with others? As a follower of Christ, what words might you offer each one of our friends?

OR, if you prefer, talk about your own experiences instead of the characters, using the same guidelines.

Carlos: Looking and touching are two different things. I mean, just because you shop doesn't mean you intend to buy anything.

Ben: Timothy and I have our tough moments. We have clashed over career, family members, cleaning the bathroom—all the big issues. But we promised to stay roommates and friends, even when things become difficult.

Timothy: My parents are twice divorced. I have had five different parents and stepparents. Ben has offered about the only stable adult relationship I've known. Lots of times I was ready to bail, but I could not stand the thought of being abandoned again or hurting Ben like that.

Chris: Lee leaves dirty socks on the couch, falls asleep in front of the television, and drinks from the gallon jug of milk rather than using a glass. He has champagne taste on a beer budget and plays opera arias constantly. Do I care? Guess who was there when my mother died? Or who listens to me complain about my job? Guess who thinks I hung the moon and gave it permission to shine? How could a few dirty socks and some high-brow music threaten that?

FINAL WORDS

Like Ruth and Naomi, God has called us into intimacy with others. Through our relationship with God through Jesus Christ and a careful consideration of biblical guidelines for intimacy, we can fashion a life with friends and spouses that resembles the peace and joy of the kingdom of God.

Final Words
In closing, summarize your insights on the topic and Scripture passages read.

If you feel that Christ has called you to a more intimate relationship, take time to make or to reaffirm your commitment, then close with this prayer: "Gracious God, who loves us unconditionally, we thank you for the gift and responsibility of intimacy. We pray we can sense you at the foundation of all our relationships so we may grow in grace with those whom we love; in the name of Jesus, who is the Christ. Amen."

COVENANT WITH CREATION

This session will explore our responsibility to the earth and our role as stewards.

GETTING STARTED

"I recycle aluminum cans, newspapers, plastics, and glass. I just built a composting center in my backyard and practice a strict vegetarian diet. We are a part of the sacred web of life and should respect all members of the earth population."

"The media talks about saving the rain forests and oceans, but it's the rain forests and oceans that save us. Without these important members of the ecosystem, human life would be impossible. Abuse them, and they will fight back. It is already happening. Ebola, a lethal virus that basically liquefies the human body, emerged when humans invaded the rain forests with saws and tractors. Mother Nature can be an unforgiving woman when provoked."

"This 'web of life' propaganda grates on my nerves. It's survival of the fittest, pure and simple. God placed all these things on the planet for our use, so what's the big deal? We were given authority over nature, not nature over humans."

Getting Started
Read the three opening statements. For each statement, respond to these questions: What ideas in each statement do you affirm? What ideas would you challenge? Which statement most reflects your own understanding?

The last decade has brought a heightened appreciation of the interconnectedness of all living things. Sadly, such awareness has not lead to significant decreases in pollution, deforestation, animal experimentation, natural resource management, overpopulation, and killing animals for sport. Can the Bible help redirect this human tendency to place our personal creature comforts over the comforts of all of God's creatures? In this session we will explore how the notion of covenant can inform our role as stewards of the earth.

STEWARDS AS GOD'S EARTH-BOUND MANAGERS

Within the Old and New Testaments, the word often translated as "steward" means "overseer" or "manager" of another person's property. For instance, in Genesis 39:1-6, Joseph becomes the steward of the house of Potiphar. While holding this role, Joseph protects the homeowner's belongings and attempts to increase the value of the home on behalf of the master. Likewise, when the term appears in Luke 16:1-9, the dishonest steward attempts to increase the value of the household prior to his termination by having debtors pay at least portions of their outstanding bills.

In Genesis 1:28-30, God employs man and woman as stewards of the earth that God just created. The pronouncement "Be fruitful and multiply" refers not only to the task of human reproduction (as is commonly thought) but to the larger job of stewardship: multiply the value and worth of all creation. In fact, the text implies that humans should reproduce simply to have enough hands to manage God's household

Stewards as God's Managers
BIBLE
Read Genesis 39:1-6. What duties characterize Joseph's work as a steward? Describe a time in your life when you were asked to "steward" the property or belongings of another person. Why do we need "managers" in the workplace? In the home?

Read Luke 16:1-9, the story of the dishonest steward. In what way was the manager shrewd? Why would the master praise the manager for such behavior? The story suggests followers of God should use the wealth of physical world to prepare for the future. As Christians, how might we be more "shrewd" in our work with others?

called Earth. Rather than understanding "subdue" or "have dominion over" in a modern context of governance, or even exploitation, we are called to practice a life of in-gathering: the accounting for all of God's created order, administering its welfare, and increasing its value until God decides to "terminate our employment"; that is, to end human life on earth.

Psalm 8 reminds the ancient and modern readers that human dignity resides within fulfillment of the responsibilities of earthly stewardship (see especially verses 6-8). Our value as humans relies on how well we manage God's world. These words seem difficult to hear, especially if we believe that simply treating one another with goodness, respect, and dignity should grant us our divine reward. But we must realize that God called humankind to manage the earth not for reward; it is merely part of the job of being human.

THE EARTH MANAGER'S CONTRACT WITH GOD

Genesis 9:1-17, known as the Noahic Covenant, can be understood as a contract between the managers (humankind) and the owner of Earth (God). We promise to fill (but not overpopulate) the planet. All living things will know instinctively of our managerial responsibilities. We may eat both plants and most animals, but only to the degree necessary for survival. We promise to revere and honor all life ("lifeblood"), including the life (blood) of other human beings. God agrees never again to destroy the entire world by water. A rainbow reminds us that God continues to evaluate our work as managers.

Pretty straightforward agreement.

Read Genesis 1:28-30. What do "subdue" and "have dominion" mean to you? Where do you see "dominion" and what forms does it take? What connections do you see between population growth and care of the earth? What concrete steps should humans take to regulate population growth? How should Christians determine the value of each of these steps?

SMALL GROUP

Ask somebody to read Psalm 8 aloud. This ancient text was probably performed as a song during worship over twenty-four hundred years ago. Try designing a "rap" or chanted version of this ancient song, to be performed at the end of the session. Or ask the more musically inclined members to set these ancient words to a modern tune.

SMALL GROUP

The Earth Manager's Contract

As a group, write a "contract" with God concerning Earth Care. Be specific about the duties, responsibilities, and tasks your group will undertake for the next three weeks to improve the environment. What special needs do you have of God to promote the success of this contract?

Once the group has agreed on the contract, write it on a large sheet of paper and post it in a prominent place. Review this contract each week when you gather.

Unfortunately, this contract appears more and more difficult to uphold. Many persons interpret this biblical text as granting permission to rob the earth of its precious resources for the sake of making the lives of a few countries comfortable while the rest of Earth-kind suffers.

Look Closer
Read Genesis 1:26-31; 2:15-17; and 9:1-17. Both are covenants concerning Creation that give humankind dominion over the earth and set boundaries for right living within that covenant. Compare the covenants to see how they are alike and different.
What are the responsibilities and expectations placed on humankind? What does God promise to do and not to do?

PSALMS: PUTTING THE CONTRACT TO MUSIC

Psalms
Ask group members to bring a hymnal from a local church to the session. For variety, borrow hymn books from many different denominations. Spend time looking in each hymnal for references to the Psalms. How many are set to music? In what other ways are the Psalms used in the hymnal? What role do the Psalms play in modern worship?

It seems our ancestors-in-faith knew the necessity of reminding each other about the responsibilities of Earth Care. For centuries faith communities utilized the psalms within the context of worship and prayer to claim our role as managers and affirm God's position as owner.

The hymns of Earth Care and creation appear frequently throughout the collection. Psalm 104:10-23, for instance, sings of the harmony that exists among all God's creatures. Psalms 8:6 declares humans as partners with God in caring for creation. Our ancestors knew of the need to be managers of the planet.

LOOKING FOR SOLUTIONS

So what can we do to reclaim our role as managers? Listen to the suggestions of Brad, LaTonyia, Jacob, and Stephanie:

Brad: The problem is greed: people using more than they need. We need to scale our lives down to the bare minimum; live in smaller communities; eat as low on the food chain as possible; distribute the risks of nuclear waste, pollution, and deforestation equally; and mandate that those persons who live beyond the bare minimum be taxed heavily.

LaTonyia: Brad's solution sounds like we would all live as monks or something. I think we should all share—you know, spread the wealth. Nobody is going to go back to the Stone Age, so to speak, so good management of the Earth's resources means all persons have equal and fair access to the same amount of resources. Then the greed

> **Looking for Solutions**
> Read each statement. What ideas can you affirm? If you could ask each of our friends one question, what would it be? Individually, then as a large group, write down your ideas for improving Earth Care.
>
> What experience do you have in Earth Care? Do you recycle, reuse, or exercise other prudent care?
>
> CASE STUDY

Ask each person to think about the place where he or she spends the most time during the day (probably work, school, or home). What are the areas of greatest waste of resources? greatest abuse? greatest opportunity for good stewardship?

What policies, programs, and decisions encourage you in those places to be the best steward you can? What practices or attitudes are the most discouraging? What can you do to reduce the negative and promote the positive?

problem would be solved. Look, if the world is a gift, we should make sure everybody benefits from it equally.

Jacob: Excuse me, Brad and LaTonyia, but you sound like time travelers from the Sixties. The system we have now works if we all practice three simple actions: reuse, renew, and recycle. We have to live a life dedicated to replenishing what we have taken. Plant more trees. Grow a vegetable garden. Use science to repair the ozone layer, increase crops' yields, discover new energy sources, and recycle everything we now discard as trash. Make landfills obsolete. Our problem: we don't want to spend the time and money it would take to change things.

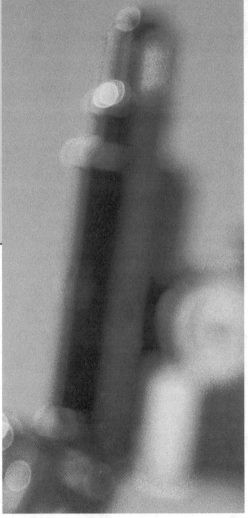

Stephanie: We cannot hide from the problems facing the earth nor can we simply sustain our current practices of pollution and destruction. In just a matter of years, our system of living will fall apart. It makes me sad to think that our shortsightedness will bring about our own destruction. Our planet will die because we refused to change our way of life.

CHURCHES AS EARTH CARE CENTERS

The apostle Paul writes throughout his letters about the unity of creation and the fulfillment of redemption within the created order. Romans 8:19-23 uses images of "bondage to decay" and "freedom of the glory of the children of God" (verse 21) to indicate the on-going covenant God has with all of creation. What has fallen into decay (creation and its creatures) will one day be redeemed. He goes on to acknowledge that "we ourselves . . have the first fruits of the Spirit." When the Spirit is at work, the whole of creation has hope.

DISCUSS

Churches as Earth Care Centers
What are the signs of decay and the signs of restoration within your church (in its identity as a "creature" within creation)? What are the signs of decay in the rest of creation that your church is addressing?

What kind of Earth Care center is your church? Take an inventory of the ways in which the church models good stewardship of resources, including people.

Biblical Studies 101: Paul and Creation

This Romans passage speaks actually of two times: the current age in which all of creation, the earth and all its creatures, exist in a state of decay and the future age in which God will reclaim and restore the entire creation in God's glory.

The idea of decay derives from Genesis 3:17-19 in which the earth is cursed as a result of the sin of the first man and woman. Paul sees this condition of decay as impermanent. By God's action through the Spirit and through the designated caretakers of the earth acting as faithful stewards, this restoration is possible on both levels.

In the current age, we who have "the first fruits of the Spirit" have the obligation to exercise those fruits for the common good (8:28-29). In the coming age, all bondage will be broken and redeemed (8:19-21).

Likewise, Christian communities should be called by God through Jesus Christ into a new lifestyle that takes seriously the responsibility of Earth Care. While our friends Brad, LaTonyia, Jacob, and Stephanie point out both the possibilities and hardships of caring for the planet, the church should foster the type of community that takes the challenge of Earth Care seriously. For a local church to become an instrument that fosters hope for salvation, it must understand that salvation extends to the earth, not just to its inhabitants. As the embodiment of the church, we must become managers chosen by God to offer environmental renewal and stewardship for all.

LAST WORDS

The Earth is a huge gift from God and its care is the principle occupation of humankind. Wise management; not only preserving, but increasing the value of creation, is the task of the wise manager, and even the dishonest steward attempted as much in his own way. What then, do the rest of us do to enhance, rather than destroy, God's dwelling for us?

CLOSING PRAYER

Closing Prayer: Form a circle. Ask a group member to read the closing prayer. If anyone is called to a greater covenant of stewardship, take time in prayer to affirm that commitment.

Endurance, cleanliness, strength, and purity. God calls us to lead lives that demonstrate these qualities. God gave us Jesus as a model to follow. But God also calls us to help the earth show these qualities as well. May our work as Earth Managers reflect a good purpose, a single truth and a respect for all living things. Amen.

LIVING WITH RULES

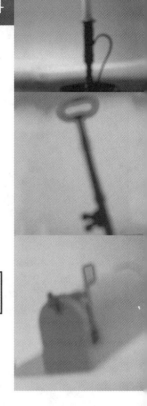

> This session will examine the biblical models of rules and how we identify what is authoritative in our own lives.

GETTING STARTED

All covenants and contracts involve rules, those guidelines that participants agree to follow. The Old and New Testaments seem full of rules and regulations. How should modern-day Christians understand such codes, ordinances, and commandments? Should Christians follow every rule established in Scripture, the workplace, and home? This session will explore the nature of rules and their meaning for our lives as believers in Jesus Christ.

START

Getting Started
Suggestion: Ask your local pastor to attend this session to participate in the exercises, answer questions about rules within the church, and to celebrate Holy Communion with participants at the end of the session.

THREE BIBLICAL MODELS FOR FOLLOWING RULES

While many Christians believe that God alone establishes the rules by which humans should live, the Old and New Testaments offer a variety of responses. Exodus 24 suggests three different ideas concerning rule formation for the wandering people of Israel.

Exodus 24:1-2, 9-11 tells of Moses and seventy religious elders approaching the throne of God to receive the Law, implying that God established the *rules only for the religious leaders*. The people simply follow the instructions of leaders. But Exodus 24:3-8 tells a different story: Moses gives the Law of God *directly to the people* (the faith community) who enter into a special relationship with God as followers of the Law. Living by the rules makes the faith community unified. And Exodus 24:12-14 describes the Law and commandments as a *gift* to God's people.

Biblical Studies 101:
Different Versions, Same Story
Exodus 24 serves as a terrific example of several writers telling a similar story in different ways. Written over a period of several hundred years, each retelling attempts to make the covenant pertinent to the readers of its day. In one story (24:1-2, 9-11) only Moses and the chosen religious leaders partake in a covenant meal and ceremony, suggesting a need to tell this ancient event in a way that bestowed total authority on religious leaders.

In a second (and perhaps later) version (24:3-8), all of the people participate in the ceremony, suggesting a time in history when the authority of following a covenant rested with all members of the faith community. By saving both versions of the story, the ancient editors of the Bible hope to tell readers of the long and hard struggle concerning the question of religious authority.

(1) FOLLOW LEADERS, NOT RULES (EXODUS 24:1-2; 9-11)

In Option One, the rules of the covenant would be pronounced and clarified by the religious leader(s). The members of the religious community would simply follow the instructions of the leaders. Many churches, families, businesses, and governments operate under this assumption. Listen to our friends Carol, Jorge, and Simon discuss this option for fashioning rules.

Carol: I have always liked this system: somebody tells me what to do, and I do it. My parents always provided great instruction and guidance. At church, I never questioned my Sunday school teachers or pastor, but listened attentively to their wisdom. And I find myself looking for a spouse who will provide that same level of direction for my life. I find comfort in the idea that God's rules are clear for those who will simply read the Bible.

Jorge: My life experience is different: I have always challenged authority figures. Nobody is responsible for my life but me. Anytime religious authority becomes absolute, there is corruption. I left my family's church because the pastor told me if I did not follow their rules I would suffer the consequences throughout eternity. Now I belong to a church that encourages me to figure out the rules for myself. I like the freedom, although the responsibility can at times feel overwhelming.

Simon: I choose the middle ground. We must follow some rules while we question others. If everybody acted like Carol, we would be like robots for God. But if every-

CASE STUDY

Follow Leaders, Not Rules
(Exodus 24:1-2; 9-11)
In pairs, review the statements of Carol, Jorge, and Simon. Write on a piece of paper four feelings raised by each statement. Write down two ideas you like about each. Then write down two things about each position you dislike. Write a haiku, a brief 17 syllable, three-line poem that expresses insight and humor, for each position. Read your terrific poetry to the larger group. Discuss the questions each poem raises.

body thought like Jorge, church would be a leaderless group of individuals and there would be no power in God's Word. Some laws, like the rules that govern nature and physics, cannot be violated. But the rules established for congregations by leaders should be reviewed with regularity to see if they serve the interests of the majority of the people. We should keep leaders who help more than they hurt and remove leaders who do more damage than good.

(2) RULES BUILD SACRED COMMUNITY (EXODUS 24:3-8)

In Option Two, the rules of the covenant would be determined by all members of the faith community. Everybody would be held accountable to the same rules. The process of identifying and shaping the rules by which God's people should live bring the people together in a way no other task could accomplish. If everybody had input in shaping the sacred rules, then nobody would have an excuse for violating them.

While this option has appeal, it does present two basic problems. First, how does a group reach consensus on its rules? For instance, how would a church determine whether the Bible should be read literally, historically, metaphorically, or through doctrine (church teachings)? Some denominations hold regular gatherings of hundreds of representatives to make such determinations. Other denominations deal with this question on a church-by-church basis. But consensus formation takes time and can be complicated, especially in a large group.

Second, how should a church enforce its

Rules Build Sacred Community (Exodus 24:3-8)

DISCUSS

How does your denomination or church establish rules? Ask your pastor for help in answering this question. Share your findings with the group.

Think about the family in which you were raised. How did the family design rules? In what ways do your current experiences of work, church, school, or family differ from this early system?

Should everybody within a community keep the same rules? Explain. Do you feel obligated to follow all the rules of your community? Explain.

In what ways might Christians be asked to live by a "different" set of rules? What are the rules for Christian communities?

rules? While the writer of Matthew tells us that Jesus instructed Peter to forgive a church member "seventy-seven" times (Matthew 18:21-22) for their wrongdoings, it seems unlikely that most churches would tolerate endless violations of rules and teachings. Some churches have review boards to address the behaviors of its members. Other faith communities rely on the clergy to determine when a member should be reprimanded. And other parishes simply ignore the violators in hopes they will choose to leave on their own accord.

(3) RULES DEMAND INDIVIDUAL RESPONSIBILITY (EXODUS 24:12-14)

In Option Three, the covenant comes to humankind as a gift, given freely by God. As a result, each person has the responsibility to decide how to respond to the covenant. Some persons may enter faith communities. Others may turn to a life of service. And still others may choose not to respond at all. But each response represents the free choice of the individual. God accepts those persons who accept the invitation of covenant while patiently loving the rest. But God never forces compliance.

Rules Demand Individual Responsibility (Exodus 24:12-14)
Why, do you think, would God give us rules if we were not obligated to follow them?

Why might God prefer persons to choose freely the life of faith?

Again, the idea sounds great. But gifts can usually be used any way the recipient desires. Some gifts are treasured while others (like Christmas fruitcakes in my family) either are quietly disposed of or wrapped again for next Christmas. The same fruitcake has made its rounds between my brothers and sisters for the last ten years.

Should the fate of the sacred covenant of God be identical to the family fruitcake?

Can every person or church determine the usefulness of the gift of a covenant in a different way? And why would human freedom be given as much importance as God's desire to be in relationship with us?

FOLLOWING RULES

Why do we follow rules? Exodus 24 offers three reasons. But must Christians respond to the covenant (and its related rules) for the same reason? Do men and women look at rules and covenants in the same manner? While scholars and writers continue to debate these questions, we might find a few of their insights helpful as Christians.

Many psychologists, ethicists, and theologians contend that human beings follow rules for different reasons. As children, we learn to follow rules to obtain a reward or to avoid punishment from external authorities such as parents or teachers. By the time we become teens, two more reasons for rule adherence emerge: all "good" persons keep certain rules, and following rules maintains the social order of our communities and organizations.

A further reason to keep laws develops within a few folks: to dialogue the rights of individuals with the rights of the larger society, in the hope of fashioning better laws. Indeed, the legal system of the United States focuses on this conceptual understanding. And a few persons, usually late in life, decide to follow laws that reflect a universal moral principle of respect for all human beings. All other laws should be challenged.

But other scholars suggest that women generally understand rules from a perspec-

Following Rules
Please note: This section uses research from the areas of psychology and moral development. Some group members may be uncomfortable using these ideas within a Bible study. You may choose to replace this section with the alternative exercise below.

The six-level system drawn from these disciplines and expressed through a theological lens could be expressed this way:

- Level One: Follow rules to avoid hell or God's wrath
- Level Two: Follow rules to go to heaven or to gain salvation
- Level Three: Follow rules to be a good Christian or role model
- Level Four: Follow rules to maintain Christian community and life
- Level Five: Follow rules, but review rules for equality, truth, and fairness to all
- Level Six: Follow rules that promote the equality of all living things

Covenant: Making Commitments That Count

tive of caring and relationships rather than intellectual principles. Young girls follow rules established by authority figures (usually male) to assure physical and psychological survival. By adolescence, rules are followed to gain acceptance and affirmation by male authority figures and persons who affirm male ideas concerning what women "should" be. And a few adult women hold to rules only if they promote a universal sense of care among persons, regardless of gender or other differences.

Listen to Carol, Jorge, and Simon as they discuss why they follow rules.

Carol: I follow rules because I was always taught to respect my earthly father and my heavenly Father. I follow God's plan for my life because if I do not, I will suffer the consequences. And I look for relationships with persons who will look up to the same authority figures as I do: God, parents, and country. And God's rules are different from human standards, like those set by governments.

Jorge: Following rules requires fashioning rules. In every group, I first learn the official rules. Then I determine whether those rules promote my interests. If they do not, I leave. If they do, I stay. I break a rule when I think it is putting me down. That's why I left my original church.

Simon: I hate to say this, but I disagree with both Carol and Jorge. I follow rules because no society can be rule-free. We have a court system that weighs the rights

Our friends Carol, Jorge, and Simon are back. Which character comes closest to mentioning your position? Based on their responses, in which level should each one be placed?

Why should Christians follow rules? If you discovered there was no heaven or hell, would you still be a Christian? Why or why not?

Many Christians differ with one another about why one should keep rules. How should we deal with this conflict?

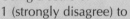
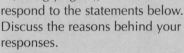

Alternative Exercise
Using a scale of 1 (strongly disagree) to 5 (strongly agree), respond to the statements below. Discuss the reasons behind your responses.

1. In my personal life, I am the one who sets the rules.
2. In my workplace, I should follow every rule established by my employer.
3. In relationships, all rules should be fashioned through discussion and consensus.
4. God demands that all the rules of the Bible be followed by Christians.
5. Under certain conditions, it is acceptable to break an established rule.
6. If you break a rule, you should be willing to adhere to the consequences.
7. You should follow rules to avoid punishment.
8. You should follow rules to gain rewards.
9. You should follow rules because that is what being a Christian is all about.
10. All rules are good.

of each individual against the principles of law. When the individual fails to demonstrate an acceptable reason for violating the law, he or she pays a fine or does time in prison. But when persons point out through their actions that a law is unjust—like what Martin Luther King, Jr. did in the Sixties—then the law is changed. And I would say the same thing about religious rules: they should promote human dignity or be rejected as flawed.

CHRIST: A FOURTH OPTION

Matthew 26:26-29 describes the Last Supper Jesus shared with his disciples. Surprisingly, Jesus borrows the blood language from Exodus 24:6-8, suggesting that the wine (as representative of Jesus' suffering) establishes a new blood covenant between God and humankind. By reading about the life, death, and resurrection of Jesus, we learn how to live our lives through the love of Christ Jesus, a new rule for a new day. By treating everybody we encounter with the same love revealed by Jesus, we can transform a world of cold rules and regulations into a kingdom of God where we are to "do justice, ... love kindness, and ... walk humbly with [our] God" (Micah 6:8).

LAST WORDS

There will always be rules. Something or someone will always have the final word. What would your life be like if the final word was always from the example of Christ?

BIBLE

Christ: A Fourth Option
Read Matthew 26:26-29. In what ways did the meal with Jesus make a difference in the lives of the disciples? In your opinion, why did the disciples choose to follow Jesus? How did this final meal bring them together as a sacred people?

With pastoral leadership, end the session with Holy Communion. Have copies of your Communion liturgy available as needed.

LOOK CLOSER

Last Words
What is your most important rule you live by? Why is it the most important? If the Scriptures are the most basic rule, how do they shape your life?

Closing Prayer
In your prayer time encourage participants who wish to invite God to rule in their lives to make their commitment, then close with the Lord's Prayer.

BROKEN PROMISES

This session is designed to investigate four biblical ideas about what to do when a covenant is broken. These models will assist group members in asking questions of forgiveness, atonement, and grace.

GETTING STARTED

Sarah: I will never forget my feelings when Chad confessed he had cheated on me. First, a wave of numbness hit me, followed by a combination of anger and disbelief. Our relationship has not been the same since.

Demi: I knew it was wrong to take office supplies home for personal use, but it seemed like everybody did it. When my supervisor brought me into the office to discuss the violation, my first impulse was to lie. Instead, I told the truth. Still, I was fired. I believe the punishment exceeded the crime.

People: Almighty and most merciful Father, we have erred and strayed from thy ways like lost sheep. We have followed too much the devices and desires of our own hearts. We have offended against thy holy laws . . . But thou, O Lord, have mercy upon us. Spare thou those, O God, who confess their faults (*The Methodist Hymnal*, 1964, 724).

Getting Started

In this session, some persons may reveal personal and possibly painful stories of their own broken promises. Keep the ambiance of the group open to confession, repentance, and reconciliation, but be very cautious of trying to do counseling.

Ask the group to divide into three smaller groups. Assign each small group one of the three statements. Each small group should read the statement aloud and discuss the following questions or instructions:

1. Specifically, what promise was broken?
2. How was the promise broken?
3. Identify the consequences of the broken promise.
4. If you had been the promise breaker, how would you feel?
5. Is there a time in your life when you felt this way?

BROKEN COVENANTS

Nobody leads a perfect life. We all break promises made to loved ones, corporations, society, and God. As Christians, we strive to keep violations to a minimum. Nevertheless, many of us have experienced the pain of broken promises. Extramarital affairs, dissolved relationships, cheating, stealing, or even broken speed limits represent different types of violations. As Christians, how should these violations be addressed? Are some violations more acceptable than others? And what role should forgiveness and grace play?

Broken Covenants
Ask the question:
Under what conditions would it be appropriate to break a covenant? Finish the following direct analogies (a thought game). Explain your responses:
- Forgiveness is like a bar of soap . . .
- Broken covenants are like leaves on a tree . . .
- God's love is like a curtain . . .

FOUR BIBLICAL IDEAS ABOUT BROKEN PROMISES

It would be nice if the Bible provided a step-by-step method by which to deal with broken promises and promise breakers. Unfortunately, the Old and New Testaments provide myriad responses to the question of violated covenants. Let's look at four possible responses found in the Bible:

1. broken covenants bring bad consequences
2. broken covenants bring bad eternity
3. broken covenants bring opportunity for forgiveness
4. broken covenants bring new covenants and healing

Four Biblical Ideas
The Bible is full of examples of broken covenants. Does this surprise you? disappoint you? please you? Explain.

Why might it be important to explore biblical ideas concerning broken covenants? What other resources would be acceptable for this investigation?

BROKEN COVENANTS BRING BAD CONSEQUENCES

Deuteronomy 28:1-19 can be summarized in two sentences: *If a community obeys its covenant with God, then it will be blessed. If a community disobeys its covenant with God, then it will be cursed.*

Known as the *Deuteronomic law*, this principle is expressed throughout much of the Old Testament. Two concepts make the Deuteronomic law pertinent to our discussion. First, the focus of the punishment or reward rests on the community, not the individual violator. While our English translation of the text uses the term "you," the original Hebrew document implies a group of people (the plural "you," or as we say in the south, "Y'all"). So individual violations of the covenant affect the larger community.

BIBLE

Bad Consequences
Read **Deuteronomy 28:1-14.** On a sheet of paper, list all the ways God blesses those communities that obey the Lord's commandments. If a person or community now shows any of these traits of "blessedness," should we assume God has indeed blessed this person or community? Explain.

Read **Deuteronomy 28:15-29.** On a second sheet of paper, list all the ways God curses those communities that disobey the Lord's commandments. If a person or community now shows any of these traits of "cursedness," should we assume God has cursed this person or community? Explain.

SMALL GROUP

Divine Justice
After reading "Biblical Studies 101," find a partner and discuss the following question:

Why do you think bad things happen to good people?

Biblical Studies 101: Divine Justice
Why does God let bad things happen to good people? Why did Job suffer so? Why is there pain and suffering in the world? Why does God allow the evil person to prosper? These questions address the biblical issue of theodicy, or divine justice. Many Old Testament books (Job, Habakkuk, Jonah, Ecclesiastes) and New Testament letters (Galatians and James) raise the question, usually arriving at different conclusions.

Job suggests that God's reasons remain elusive. Habakkuk simply reminds persons to live the life of faith, regardless of the outcome. Ecclesiastes claims everything is preordained by God, so just lie back and enjoy the ride. Paul contends God finds persons "not guilty" of covenant violations (usually described as justification) through the life of faith, while James suggests the works of Torah bring about God's reward.

DISCUSS

Describe a recent event in your life that presented you troubles you felt you did not deserve. Where was God during this turmoil? What difference did it make to you?

Second, God behaves as a dispenser of rewards and punishments, like a cosmic parent. While some persons find this version of divine justice simple and easy to understand, it does raise an important question: Why do bad things happen to good people? And why must an entire family or community suffer for the wrongs of an individual?

Closer Look

Skim through these various books of the Bible for examples of theodicy. Use a Bible commentary to aid your understanding. Theologically, are you more like Job, Habakkuk, Ecclesiastes, Paul, or James? Explain?

LOOK CLOSER

BROKEN COVENANTS BRING BAD ETERNITY

BIBLE

Bad Eternity
Form two small groups. Have one group read 2 Kings 13:1-9, the story of Jehoahaz, a bad king of ancient Israel. Ask the other group to read 2 Kings 13:10-13, about Jehoash (or Joash), a corrupt king of Judah, a nation to the south of Israel. Explore these questions: Why did the writer think the king was bad?

BIBLE

What were the "sins of Jeroboam?" Read **1 Kings 12:25-33**. Using modern language, write an obituary for your king, Jehoahaz or Joash. Be prepared to share with the larger

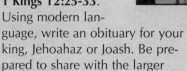

Second Kings 13 is a theological history: a traditional account of the nations of Israel and Judah based on the writer's understanding of God rather than simply reporting "the facts." How these countries, and the kings who ruled them, are remembered by the writer is based on the way the writer believes the rulers kept God's covenant. After reading this section, you will see the verdict is not very good. The kings are rotten, along with both countries. In short, those persons and communities who break covenants will be remembered throughout time as bad persons. Our deeds in life give us an opportunity to write our own obituary, the words by which we will be remembered.

We know how this principle works in our world. For instance, the name *Hitler* brings to mind images of death, murder, and demonic forces in the world. The name *Martin Luther King, Jr.*, however, appears synonymous with civil rights, justice, and equality. Depending on how we lead our life of faith, we will be remembered as good, bad, or (perhaps worst) not at all. The Christian witness calls us to be a memorable relative in the family of God.

BROKEN COVENANTS BRING OPPORTUNITY FOR FORGIVENESS

Isaiah 40–55 represents a section of the Old Testament known as Second Isaiah. Written at the end of the Babylonian Exile (587–539 B.C.), Second Isaiah begins with words of *forgiveness*. Read Isaiah 40:1-2. Apparently the writer assumed the Babylonian Exile occurred as a result of a broken covenant (reflecting the Deuteronomic law idea mentioned above). But the writer also believes God forgave the exiled people of Jerusalem because they engaged in appropriate *acts of contrition* (admitting guilt) and *penance* (repairing the wrongs).

While being cast into a foreign land for forty years may sound rather extreme, the writer does illustrate that forgiveness is not cheap. Many Christians suggest the death of Jesus as the ultimate way in which God helped humankind repair the wrongs committed against their promises with God. Even so, Christians are expected to admit when they have broken a promise and make amends. Determining the appropriate amends, however, has always been a difficult matter.

If you were asked to write your own obituary, what would it say? What would be the verdict on your life?

Come back together as a large group. First read aloud your modern obits of the kings. Then share insights and comments concerning the last question.

Opportunity for Forgiveness
Read **Isaiah 40:1-5**. Ask the group to consider the following questions:

When have you experienced "Exile moments," those times of exclusion because you broke a promise?

What behavior do you think demonstrates contrition and penance?

At what point did you receive forgiveness? If you did not receive forgiveness, why was it withheld?

Closer Look
Read the three descriptions of atonement and the related Scripture in "Biblical Studies 101." Why do you think Jesus died on the cross? What concrete difference does the death make in your Christian life?

Ask your pastor about these three models. Most Christian traditions affirm all three approaches to explaining the death and resurrection of Jesus.

BROKEN COVENANTS BRING NEW COVENANTS

New Covenants
Read **Romans 11:1-16** for details. When would leaving a friendship, job, or marriage promote healing and wholeness with both parties involved? What issues would need to be considered before breaking a relationship? Have you been in a position in which breaking the promise was the most healthy, positive thing to do? What was that like?

In a letter to the Christian community in Rome, written approximately thirty years after the death of Jesus, Paul uses numerous references to the Old Testament to explain how God allowed the Jews of ancient times to break their covenant with God so God could enter a relationship with the non-Jew, or Gentile. Through belief in the teaching, death, and resurrection of Jesus rather than the old laws of Torah, the Gentiles would develop a dynamic relationship with God. In turn, the Jewish communities of the day would be reminded of their possibility of intimacy with God and return with great vigor to keeping the ancient covenant. So by breaking an old covenant, a new covenant can arise.

We often find that covenants (relationships) we entered with good intention no longer work. Friendships dissolve. Marriages fail. We leave our church for another faith community (or none at all).

According to Paul's reasoning, however, one would normally not break a covenant unless doing so could promote healing and wholeness with both parties involved. Obviously, this model requires a great deal of discussion, introspection, and clarity concerning the nature of relationships and what a positive future might be.

THE CASE OF DIFFERENCES

Read the following story about Kimberly and Sebastian.

To their friends, Kimberly and Sebastian said it was "love at first sight." Three years ago, when they met at a professional conference, life became magical. As if they had known each other their entire lives, Kimberly and Sebastian exhibited instant trust and affection. Within the year, Sebastian had moved across the country to be closer to Kimberly. The couple married exactly twelve months from their first meeting.

But then the relationship changed. Work responsibilities made heavy demands on both Sebastian and Kimberly. Conflict became more commonplace. Kimberly began to express political and religious views different from those of Sebastian, who tended to reject these opinions as ill-informed. The couple spent time talking to their pastor and attending several sessions of marriage counseling. But enough was enough. Last week, Kimberly moved into an apartment, leaving Sebastian with their small home and the dog.

CASE STUDY

A Case of Differences
Read the case study carefully or present one (perhaps a real life situation) suggested by a group member. Ask these questions: What are the specific issues at stake in the case of Kimberly and Sebastian (or the main parties)? Make a list of these issues on a large sheet of paper.

Look at the list. First as individuals, then as a group, list the issues in order of importance, with the most important issue labeled #1, the second most important issue as #2, and so on. Discuss what ideas or principles informed your priorities.

If you could speak to each character, what would you say?

PUTTING THE PIECES TOGETHER

CASE STUDY

Read the section **"Putting the Pieces Together"**. Respond to the six questions while reflecting on the case study. If time permits, use the six questions to reflect on a time in your life when you considered leaving a job, church, friendship, or marriage. What role did any of these seven questions play in your process of discernment?

While God wishes us happiness and joy, our relationships with others can often bring hardship. But the prospect of difficulty should not lead us to either avoid relationships or believe that God simply "has it in for us." Instead, Christian faith asks us to consider the following questions:

1. What will be the real consequence of breaking a covenant with this person?
2. At what point would breaking a promise be either ethical or moral?
3. How do I wish to be remembered when I have died? What will be my legacy?
4. How do I admit to breaking a promise?
5. In what concrete ways can I repair the damage I caused to others?
6. When should a relationship be terminated? Under what conditions?
7. What does my faith (Bible, prayer life, and so on) suggest I should do?

CLOSING PRAYER

CLOSE

Closing Prayer
Review the group's feelings and insights on broken covenants. Be sure that anyone who revealed a personal, and perhaps painful, story has been cared for. If any one feels called by God to renew or review a particular covenant, ask for prayers for those participants, then close with the printed prayer.

O God, you receive me like a forgiven child; into your arms I run. O God, you love me like a partner in life; beside you I shall stand. O God, you remember me like a grandparent; in you I shall rest forever. Amen.

MAKING SACRIFICES

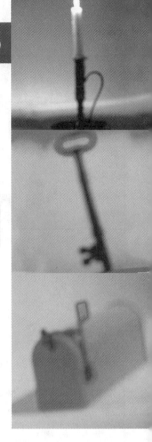

This session explores the nature of Christian sacrifice and its relationship to our daily lives.

GETTING STARTED

"When Chip and I started dating, we discovered the need to make sacrifices. It was no longer just about me. I had to consider what might be best for both of us. Now that we plan to be married we will have to sacrifice space, privacy, and some of our independence."

"Sacrifice only counts if what you surrender lowers your quality of life. For example, I joined an international peace movement for two years and lived in a small village in the former Soviet Union, teaching English as a second language. Life was rustic at best. But the sacrifices I made brought incredible rewards."

"It is hard to imagine giving up anything. I mean, I work hard for the things I own and the friends I have. How would changing my lifestyle help anybody else? God gave me the blessings of a good house, car, education, and job, so who am I to doubt God?"

All covenants require some kind of sacrifice. Couples surrender privacy and time to each other. Workers may yield independence

Getting Started
Ask group members to write on a piece of paper four characteristics of sacrifice, based on their own experiences. After these individual lists have been completed, compile a common list on a large piece of paper. Post it in a prominent location, so all group members can see it easily.

Read the three opening comments on page 59. Evaluate each statement, using the common list. How many ideas of sacrifice did each statement reflect? How many characteristics did all three statements neglect? How would you define the term "Christian sacrifice?"

to their employer. College students give up quite a bit of freedom to attend an institution. But are all sacrifices necessary? How do you know if you have surrendered too much? And how should Christians understand sacrifice, especially as it relates to the life, death, and resurrection of Jesus? These questions will be explored in this session.

WHAT IS A SACRIFICE?

What Is a Sacrifice? Read Leviticus 19:1-37. After reading the Scripture, make another common list of the characteristics of holiness. How many of these ideas sound familiar? The world described in this passage was one of ancient farmlands and country living. How should the modern reader interpret these codes of holiness, especially if you live in a city?

Compare the two common lists. What ideas are found on both? Based on your common lists, how are sacrifice and holiness related?

The word *sacrifice* comes from the ancient language of Latin, suggesting "the act of making something sacred or holy." In the Old Testament, blood and grain sacrifices were performed in the Temple of God to change sinful people or conditions (like bad weather or crops) into holy and pure ones (people realigned with God). This action would restore the covenant with God to its original order.

The apostle Paul told his followers that Christ was like the "paschal lamb," an animal slaughtered for the Jewish Passover meal, sacrificed for them (1 Corinthians 5:7). The writer of Hebrews (9:11-22) describes Christ as a sacrificer (or chief priest) as well as the sacrifice in the hope of fashioning a new covenant (relationship) between God and the world.

TWENTY-FIRST CENTURY SACRIFICE

But how should modern-day Christians understand sacrifice, the act of making something sacred? First, Christians worldwide proclaim the death of Jesus as a central event. By dying on a cross, Jesus suffered for his beliefs, practices, and teachings. Paul understood this central idea when he informed the small assembly of believers in Thessalonika that suffering pain and persecution in the name of Christ resembles the actions of true followers of Jesus (1 Thessalonians 1:6-8; 3:6-10). Standing for what one knows as truth can be risky. Christian sacrifice can involve standing by the truth of the Gospel, even if ridiculed for your decision.

Second, Christian sacrifice promotes *holiness*, a term that describes a specific relationship with God, available through Jesus. In this relationship, Christians "provoke one another to love" (Hebrews 10:24). Because we have been introduced to God by Jesus, we behave differently than other

Discuss the "Biblical Studies 101" box.
What does it mean for Christians today to speak of the blood of Jesus? Some Christians understand the word to imply that Jesus offered his life as a substitution for our own. Others contend that Jesus paid a ransom with his own life so humankind could be free. And other Christians believe "blood" refers to the moral example Jesus provided through his life. Discuss these interpretations of the "blood of Jesus" in groups of two. Identify the strengths and concerns of each. Personally, how do you understand the death of Jesus?

Twenty-first Century Sacrifice
Tell a story about when you stood up for your beliefs, even when doing so was not popular. During this time, where did you find your strength? How did the situation end?

folks, even when the rest of the world seems to have lost its mind.

SMALL GROUP

Bring to the session a recent newspaper or news magazine. Ask each group member to remove from the publication an article that describes a local, regional, national, or world event. Ask each group member to read their article carefully. With a pen or marker, each person should highlight those words that reflect persons experiencing sacrifice, the act of making something holy or sacred. If not found, spend a few moments writing an additional paragraph to the article, suggesting how sacrifice might have been shown in the situation. As a large group, share your findings.

PROVOKING RELATIONSHIPS

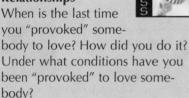
Provoking Relationships
When is the last time you "provoked" somebody to love? How did you do it? Under what conditions have you been "provoked" to love somebody?

What does "provoke one another to love" mean? Should we prod our dear friends and companions with sticks, or perhaps issue the threat, "Hey, enter a loving covenant with me or else!"? Fortunately, the writer of Hebrews meant neither idea. Instead, Christians provoke others to love by promoting kindness, performing good deeds, attending church, and building the kingdom of God (Hebrews 10:25). But how can these acts be considered sacrificial? Remember, sacrifice means to make something holy. When you "provoke" others through living a Christian life, you treat them as the most precious of God's creations. This lifestyle can become quite difficult when persons fail to treat you with the same respect. Just listen to Lisa's tale of woe:

CASE STUDY
Read Lisa's tale of woe or ask a volunteer to raise a similar experience for the group to discuss. As a group, identify the "love-busting" actions. How might the situation be resolved to "provoke" loving among all the characters?

"Last night was going fine. Robert and I had just returned from class. There was a knock on the door and two of Robert's friends walked in. Now, while I don't really

62

care for these guys, I know Robert likes them, so I decided to say nothing and be kind and gracious. Well, Robert and his friends start talking about the "old days" of high school, leaving me just sitting there. I did not know Robert back then, nor did I care for a trip down Memory Lane. By the time this 'bonding session' ended, it was too late to discuss my virtual exclusion from most of the evening. I just wish Robert would show me more respect."

Both Lisa and Robert could use a lesson in the art of Christian provocation. Treating somebody as the most precious of God's creations sounds so nice, but is it really possible? And what about forgiveness? Should Lisa simply forget Robert's insensitivities? How does forgiveness serve as an act of sacrifice? Read on and find out.

BACK TO HEBREWS

The New Testament Book of Hebrews expressed the views of many early Christians who believed that reality existed on two levels: the physical world and the spiritual world. The physical world, a mere "shadow and no true image" of the spiritual realm (Hebrews 10:1-25) calls the faithful disciples of Jesus Christ to act as if they are already living in the spiritual world. Through this radical lifestyle, called faith, one would have access to Christ's forgiveness while being required to forgive others. To make sacrifices for others on the earthly dimension—through good works and deeds—serves as an important way of linking the two realms. Christ makes this sacrificial life of forgiveness possible.

Back to Hebrews
Read Hebrews 10:1-25
BIBLE
and use a commentary to help explain the text. What, do you think, is the difference between sacrifice as making something holy and sacrifice as giving up something? Give an example to show your understanding of the difference. How do you understand the relationship between the physical and the spiritual? What would it mean to protect and honor the spirit of another person? What conditions makes forgiveness difficult? How can we overcome these difficulties?

Review the chart of Sacrifice Builders and Busters on page 64. What other ideas would you add to the chart?

BACK TO RELATIONSHIPS

SMALL

GROUP

Back to Relationships
Divide the group into three smaller teams. Ask each team to write a response to Ray, Charlene, or Yolanda, based on their understanding of covenant and Christian sacrifice. Each team should select a different character. After a few moments, return to the larger group and share your responses.

To sacrifice means to make something holy through good deeds and abundant forgiveness because you honestly believe that doing so will bring about the kingdom of God. But putting Christian sacrifice into action can be harder than it sounds. Listen to Ray, Charlene, and Yolanda discuss Christian sacrifice.

Ray: Yeah, the Christian life asks a lot of me. Like some Sundays, I don't want to go to church, but I go anyway. Once I get there, I drink coffee with my church friends, study the Bible, and attend worship. Afterwards, I feel charged for the week.

Charlene: Oh Ray, you don't understand the real meaning of Christian sacrifice. We are asked to duplicate the lives of Jesus' disciples: live simply and love greatly, even when life gets rough or love feels difficult. And we are to love all persons, just not those persons who happen to show up at the coffee pot on Sunday morning. Much of my time is spent helping others. I live on a tight budget so I can use my resources to assist those persons who struggle to survive.

Yolanda: Look, Charlene, I am busy raising two children and working two jobs. I don't have the time to commit my life to working miracles. I look at Christian sacrifice this way: Jesus died for my sins so I can have a chance at eternal life. No guarantees, but a chance. I treat people with respect and attempt to do the right thing. But if "sacrifice" means attending church and living in poverty, I think the church is in big trouble. And Ray, try thinking about somebody other than yourself; that seems to be an essential part of sacrifice.

SACRIFICE IN THE WORLD

Now we have identified the characteristics of Christian sacrifice and explored how they might be applied to relationships. These principles can help us identify and address the problems in our communities and world as well. Let's look at the town of Holingsbrook, where the citizens are struggling over a critical and emotional issue.

Sacrifice in the World
How should the church teach persons about Christian sacrifice?

Describe some famous people who you believe demonstrated Christian sacrifice in action. What additional qualities made them memorable figures?

Must a person be a Christian to demonstrate the principles of Christian sacrifice? Explain your response.

A Case Study on Sacrifice
STUDY   Read the following case study carefully. Then discuss the case using the following instruction.

Make a list of all the characters in the case study. Are there important persons or communities implied but not directly mentioned in the case?

Next to the name of each character, write the issues of the case from their perspective. Some persons, agencies, or communities might have more than one issue.

Review the characteristics of Christian sacrifice. Look at your list one more time. Considering each character (or entity) separately, how, if they were to enact the principles of Christian sacrifice, might they solve the problem at hand?

Spend a few moments describing how you would resolve the tensions in Holingsbrook. What principles or ideas informed your solution?

A CASE STUDY ON SACRIFICE

Hollingsbrook, a mid-size city of fifty-six thousand citizens, ended the year in a crisis. The state legislature had decided to locate the new high-security prison on the edge of the city. The new prison would stand within one mile of the low-rent housing district on the south of town, known by most Hollingsbrook citizens as the "undesirable" part of town.

While the prison would bring many needed jobs to the area, many persons were concerned with having convicted felons living within a mile of the city. Others believed the location of the prison would hurt South Hollingsbrook by making bad living conditions worse. Their solution: relocate the prison to a larger percentage of the population (regardless of socioeconomic status) and let them assume the risk.

Another gathering of persons rejected the idea of the prison completely, saying, "Sure, we need more prisons, but not in my neighborhood." Still others objected to the idea of incarceration on moral grounds: "The United States imprisons more of its citizens than any other nation in the Western hemisphere. This injustice must end."

CLOSING PRAYER

Gracious and loving God, you brought forth Jesus to teach the world about Christian sacrifice. Help us remember our responsibility to live this day as if the kingdom of God has already arrived. Amen.

Closing Prayer
Spend a moment in silence asking God about how you can best make your own sacrifice, then pray together the closing prayer.

RENEWING OUR COVENANT WITH GOD

This session is designed to explore the sabbath and solitude as two ways to renew our relationship with God.

GETTING STARTED

Sharon: Sometime during the day I find a few minutes to spend time with God. Usually that time starts with a prayer of thanksgiving, then prayers for everyone who needs to sense God's closeness. Then I use a devotional guide my pastor gave me to read the daily Scripture passage and think about how that passage gets me through the day.

Avery: Once a month, I pack the car and head to the woods for the weekend. There is a special spot: deep woods, babbling brook, and fresh mountain air. I swear God speaks to me through that special place. For a moment, I feel the Holy Spirit descend, fill-

Getting Started
Your group may choose to gather for this session in a natural setting or a location removed from the rubble of everyday life.

Read aloud the statements of Sharon, Avery, Leipold, and Twyla. After each statement has been read, ask the entire group, "What question would you ask this person about renewing their relationship with God?" List these questions on a large piece of paper.

Provide group members an opportunity to respond creatively to their favorite of the four comments (or one of the questions asked of that fictional person) by fashioning an artistic expression using construction paper, glue, scissors, magazines, markers, and pens. As each person finishes his or her work of art, afix it to a wall or other flat service with masking tape, creating a "Gallery of Renewal." When the gallery is completed, invite group members to generate titles for each work of art. Be sure to ask persons to explain the meaning behind the suggested title.

ing me with grace and love. By the end of the weekend, I usually have placed the problems of my life in a new perspective, thanks to God.

Leipold: My life is so hectic. I don't have time for daily devotionals or woodsy retreats. But come Sunday morning, I give the entire day to the glory of God. From a morning of church praise and study, to an afternoon of singing hymns and a prayer vigil, through an evening of worship and meditation, Jesus becomes my only point of focus. What a charge for the week.

Twyla: I left the church many years ago. But my faith calls me to help build the kingdom of God. So twice a week I spend two hours in the afternoon either sorting and labeling clothes for the local clothing bank or fixing dinner at the shelter. By becoming the hands, head, and heart of Jesus, I keep my promise to make the world a better place.

All sacred covenants require times of renewal and remembrance. Without renewal, relationships can begin to feel stale, tired, and boring. Do Christians have certain ways in which to recharge relations with others, our world, and God? What clues does the Bible offer? This session explores how we can rejuvenate our covenant with others.

SABBATH: SACRED TIME WITH GOD

Most Christians will describe Sunday as *sabbath*, that one day of the week we remember the mighty acts of God in the world, especially through the Creation. But the Bible describes many different sabbath events.

Sabbath: Sacred Time
Ask for volunteers to read each Scripture passage aloud. Ask the group to reflect on the following questions for each passage:
- How would you describe the meaning of sabbath in the passage?
- What special characteristics could you attribute to this idea of sabbath?
- When in your life have you experienced this type of sabbath moment?

Covenant: Making Commitments That Count

An ancient word meaning "to abstain or cease," *sabbath* referred to the first shift from creating to living (Genesis 2:2-3); a sacred day of praying and celebrating God's presence in the world (Deuteronomy 5:12-15); every seventh year (Leviticus 25:1-7); a special year of renewal with God (Deuteronomy 31:9-13); and the many years of the Babylonian Exile, during which God's sacred land found renewal and restoration (2 Chronicles 36:20-21). Regardless of the length of time, sabbath is a time of renewal.

But renewal requires work. Historically, sabbath has always been an active, but dramatic shift of attention from ordinary time to sacred time. In this sense, our regular schedule—and not we—takes a "rest" so our sacred schedule can emerge. Acts of sabbath should align our soul with the heart of God by abstaining or ceasing our regular routine. Through prayer, worship, meditation, praise, song, dance, and Bible study, our very lives can focus on reclaiming the meaning of our covenant with God through Jesus Christ. The comments from Sharon and Leipold mirror this idea of sabbath.

LIVING JUBILEE!

Every fiftieth year, known also as the Jubilee (Leviticus 25:8-55) marked a sacred time within the hopes and dreams of God's people. Through radical acts of compassion, peace, and justice, all life was to be given a second chance. By looking at Jubilee as a sabbath for the world, Tywla's comments concerning covenant renewal finds biblical witness. Perhaps the Christian life, as modeled by Jesus and his disciples, should focus on living toward the Jubilee.

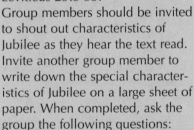

Living Jubilee!
Again, ask a volunteer to read aloud slowly Leviticus 25:8-55.
Group members should be invited to shout out characteristics of Jubilee as they hear the text read. Invite another group member to write down the special characteristics of Jubilee on a large sheet of paper. When completed, ask the group the following questions:

- Look at the list of traits of Jubilee. How would you describe each in modern language?
- What would the world be like if we lived as a "Jubilee People," followers of Christ who practiced these ideas?
- How do the practices of Jubilee compare to your understanding of the life led by Jesus and the disciples?
- What actions might we undertake to bring about Jubilee in our community?

Renewing Our Covenant With God

LOOKING FOR SABBATH MOMENTS

With hectic schedules, numerous responsibilities, and social obligations, it can be
difficult to find the sabbath moment, when
we shift from ordinary to sacred time to
renew our relationship with God. I took an
informal poll recently, asking many young
adults about how they experience the sabbath. Here are some common responses.

■ On the local golf course, early Sunday
  morning
■ Reading the paper with a cup of coffee,
  relaxing
■ Being a couch potato in front of the TV
  during the evening
■ Soaking in a hot tub, listening to a
  favorite CD
■ Being with friends

While these events sound relaxing, comfort-
ing, and rejuvenating, they fail to qualify as
sabbath moments. Remember, our personal
tranquility and restoration may be a byprod-
uct of sabbath, but the focus should be placed
upon deepening our relationship with God.

Sabbath Shapers, when practiced with
regularity, can lead us toward an experience
of sabbath moments. But what about just
spending time alone? In what way can solitude promote a sense of sabbath? What is a
sabbath moment?

Sabbath Shapers
■ Attending and participating in worship
■ Using daily devotional material
■ Reading the Bible
■ Singing praise songs with others
■ Listening to a dramatic recitation of the
  Psalms
■ Attending spiritual retreats with others
■ Experiencing Christian meditations and
  visualizations
■ Having an intentional sacred time
■ Abstaining from regular time activities
■ Falling in love with God again
■ Building the kingdom of God

Sabbath Scrapers

- Worship is boring/ the sermon was long
- What's a devotional guide?
- The Bible makes no sense to me
- Headphones and loud tunes are heavenly
- Psalms are boring old poems
- I went camping with my brother last week
- I just read a book on reducing stress
- Sabbaths are spontaneous events
- My life demands constant attention
- God has left the building/ not around
- Can't I just write a check?

SMALL GROUP

Close the ritual by inviting group members to hold hands. Say: "As long as the Christ dwells in us, we are the light to the world. We promise to work with one another to keep that holy light burning forever. Let us, with eyes and hearts open, repeat our response 'As God's people, so let it be done' ten times." Again, lead the group in the response, but speak in a slow, clear voice. Begin softly, but raise the volume with each response, until the group is shouting by the tenth round. At the end of the ritual, declare "Amen!" and initiate signs of grace and reconciliation (hugs and snugs).

SACRED SOLITUDE: LOOKING FOR GOD

Have you ever noticed how many "forty-day" events can be found in the Bible? Noah and friends weather the great flood for forty days (Genesis 7:4,17), Moses stays on Mount Sinai forty days talking with God (Exodus 24:18), and both Elijah and Jesus spend forty days in the desert (1 Kings 19:8; Matthew 4:2). The "forty-day" experiences of Noah, Moses, Elijah, and Jesus were characterized with *hardship*, *solitude*, and *a desire to respond to God*.

Each religious leader overcame enormous obstacles in order to find that precious moment of solitude in which a divine message was revealed. Like many other religious persons, these pillars of faith discovered God in the midst of separation and solitude.

DISCUSS

Sacred Solitude
Ask group members, What might be the difference between solitude and being alone?

Look at the "Gallery of Renewal" again. How do these works represent solitude?

Biblical Studies 101: Numbers Mean a Lot

In the ancient world, numbers were used to say many things. For instance, most ancient cultures used the number forty as a symbolic way to say "it took a long time and those times were sometimes rough." Other common numbers used in the Old and New Testaments include four (often meaning something universal or divine), three (often suggesting completeness), and twelve (a multiple of three and four, suggesting divine completion). So when reading the Bible, remember: numbers are always important.

Are these sacred "forty-day" encounters of God only part of our religious past? What might a "forty-day" experience look like today? How would I prepare myself for such an encounter, given my fast-paced schedule? What value would sacred solitude have for the modern-day Christian? I asked a few friends for their advice; let's hear their ideas.

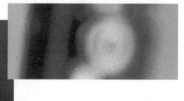

Closer Look
Look up each of the "forty-day" events in the Bible and note the context for the event as well. Then discuss the questions about these sacred "forty-day" encounters of God.

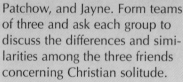

Three Voices
Ask group members to read silently the statements of Larry, Patchow, and Jayne. Form teams of three and ask each group to discuss the differences and similarities among the three friends concerning Christian solitude.

THREE VOICES

Larry: Wow! I really never thought about forty days of solitude before. But it seems to me that if we use the Bible as a guide, sacred solitude would require leaving the world behind for a while. You might even need to deny yourself of regular food, water, and sleep. I remember reading the biography of Thomas Merton, a famous Christian monk of this century. He often secluded himself from the world, looking for that mountaintop experience with God.

Patchow: I don't know about this Merton guy; I do remember hearing stories of the

72

Vision Quest from my grandfather, who was a Hopi Indian. He said to become a man, a boy would travel to an isolated spot known to be active with spirits, like a lake or mountain. There he would deny himself food and water until the spirits spoke to him. While the story always stuck with me, I am not sure it has any meaning for modern Christians.

Jayne: There is no need to take it so seriously. I think sacred solitude requires us to carve out times in our weekly schedule where we focus our total attention on God. Not our bellies. Not our minds. Not our schedules. Just God. Just be still and let God speak to you. How long should you be still? As long as you possibly can.

ANCIENT VOICES

The Sayings of the Desert Fathers, an ancient collection of Christian writings, tells of holy men and women who lived in the deserts of Egypt, Syria, Palestine, and Arabia during the fourth and fifth centuries to find God through solitude. Look at these depictions of sacred solitude.

■ The calm Christian is like a still pool of water, capable of reflecting the sun.

■ It is possible to be solitary in one's mind while living in a crowd, and it is possible for one who is solitary to live in the crowd of his own thoughts.

■ Do not be always wanting everything to turn out as you think it should, but rather as God pleases, then you will be undisturbed and thankful in your prayer.

Then the group should write its own statement about Christian solitude, which will be shared with the larger group. Be explicit, explaining what particular behaviors would bring about an experience of sacred solitude.

Bring the large group together and ask each group to present its statement. Encourage participants to ask questions and make comments about the presented statements.

Ancient Voices
Distribute index cards and ask each participant to write down one of the three sayings. Invite group members to spend about ten minutes alone, removed from the presence of other persons and distractions to reflect in silence on the wisdom of the ancient saying. Think about what Scripture informed the idea. Attempt to paraphrase the sentence. Ask God in prayer to illuminate your mind and heart concerning how your saying can challenge your spiritual life for the upcoming week

After ten minutes, invite volunteers to share their experience of solitude. What insights emerged concerning the wisdom of the Desert Fathers?

Paul: Solitude Expert
Find two maps: one of
the journeys of Paul or
of the Roman world
(which may be included in a
study Bible) and a modern map of
the world. Look first at the Bible
map. Locate the city Thessalonika.
Now locate the same city on the
modern map. Thessalonika rests
in the southern part of the Balkans
region, known by such countries
as Bosnia, Greater Serbia,
Macedonia, and Greece. Ask
group members what they know
about the current and historic
events of this region.

**Read 1 Thessalonians
5:12-26.** Look at the
list of Insider
Guidelines about
Sacred Solitude. How might your
life be altered by practicing such
principles? Why would such a
practice be identified as
"Solitude?" How might your community be different if such practices occurred? And what about
the modern day Balkans region?
What makes these simple principles so hard to follow?

Closing Prayer
Join together in the
closing prayer.

PAUL: SOLITUDE EXPERT

The Christian converts in Thessalonika
suffered the taunts and torments of out-
siders. The peace once found in Christ Jesus
quickly evaporated as daily life became
hectic and uncertain. It would take a letter
written by Paul to redirect both their hearts
and actions toward sacred solitude and
Christian community. Paul's advice to this
small assembly involved fashioning a community of sacred solitude, using these
guidelines for insiders (1 Thessalonians
5:12-26).

1. No division or disagreements among
   church members. Always do good.
2. All members within the organization
   should do the same amount of work.
3. Help one another equally.
4. Be patient.
5. Thank God for all things.
6. Use the notion of goodness to critique all
   things.
7. Pray for one another.
8. At the appropriate time during worship,
   greet each other with a kiss.

CLOSING PRAYER

Great God, your wisdom and love span
the centuries. Guide us in shaping spaces of
sacred solitude so we may feel your presence and renew our covenant with you.
Amen.

CASE STUDIES

Getting Started

Use any of these cases in place of or in addition to the cases in the sessions as a means of stimulating discussion.

The Desert

Two persons had to cross a desert. When they started, both had equal amounts of food rations and water. When they were in the middle of the desert, one person's water bag broke and all the water spilled into the sand. Both realized that if they tried sharing the remaining water, they would die of thirst. If one person had the remaining water, however, that person would probably survive.

- What should the two persons do? State your reasons.

- What issues of covenant does the case study raise?

- What difference might it make if the two persons were husband and wife? two men? two women? best friends? lovers? mere acquaintances? of a different racial or ethnic heritage? a child and an older adult? a Christian; and an atheist?

- On what grounds should value be placed on a human life? Might someone's be worth more than another's? If so, why?

- What scriptural or faith issues inform your ideas?

A Question of AIDS

Until recently, very little work had been done to educate the small town of Rock Ridge about AIDS. National and state funding for AIDS education had decreased significantly. Little was known about the extent of infection in Bellard County (Rock Ridge was the county seat) and only a few articles about AIDS had been published in the local paper. Once in awhile the television would mention that persons in some large city had been stricken with the disease, but no additional information was either offered or pursued.

Many church and civic leaders in Rock Ridge chose to believe that AIDS was a low priority, given other pressing health and development needs. Some had faith that religious beliefs would limit the spread of HIV. Others refused to acknowledge that prostitution, unprotected sex, and unsafe injections were even local problems.

That was until the local physician, Barbara Eubanks, stood up at the last City Council meeting to announce that she was currently treating six Rock Ridge citizens who had tested positive for HIV, the virus that causes AIDS. This statement was made in the middle of a request for the city to fund an AIDS program that would provide information, counseling, free condoms, clean needles, and emotional support for persons living with AIDS. The identities of the six citizens were not revealed.

After a brief period of silence, there was a huge uproar. "Who are they?" one voice cried. "This is God's way of telling us something," another chimed. "We must show compassion," the third shouted. After order returned to the proceedings, the mayor of Rock Ridge made the following statement. "By the disruption in this room, it seems clear that the City Council will require specific information concerning these six people and their particular needs before funding for any AIDS program would be approved. When you release this information, we can proceed."

■ How should Dr. Eubanks respond?

■ Under what conditions should a confidence be broken?

■ Listen to the different voices in the case: Dr. Eubanks, the mayor, the three nameless voices. How does each character understand the issue?

■ What issues of covenant are at stake? What role could or should the church play in resolving the case?

■ What scriptural or faith issues inform your ideas?

■ If a covenant is or will be broken, what might be done to restore it?

How Much Honesty?

Two young college students, Reginald and Charmane, met in chemistry class during their first year. Charmane's parents had died in a tragic car accident when she was ten; until college, she had moved from one foster family to the next. It was only due to her incredible intelligence that she received a full scholarship to attend this rather prestigious school. When Reginald asked Charmane about her personal history, she lied, "Our family has lived oversees most of our lives; in fact, my parents live currently in Brussels. My father is a wealthy European banker who believes that I should make it on my own, so I have been working to earn money and show him my independence. Of course, when I turn twenty-one, I will receive a huge sum of money from a trust fund."

Reginald came from a poor family but had the dream of going into business and becoming rich. He believed Charmane's story and saw her as a good prospect for making his dream a reality. So he spent his time—and meager savings—attempting to impress Charmane, which he accomplished. Love flourished quickly. Six months later, Reginald and Charmane married. After the honeymoon, Charmane confessed, telling Reginald the truth concerning her background. In anger, Reginald stormed from the room, swearing that he would file for divorce.

- Identify the issues raised by the case study. How would you describe the motivations of Reginald and Charmane?

- Whose actions do you consider worse? State your reasons.

- What specific issues of covenant does the case raise for you?

- On what grounds should a divorce be sought? What might be the consequences of attempting to assign blame?

- What scriptural or faith issues inform your ideas?

- What might be done to attempt to restore this covenant?

Company Secrets

Shanice and Clarence work with intellectual properties for a high-tech computer technologies firm and have access to sensitive information. Both know that conditions for continued employment include an absolute pledge of loyalty and confidentiality in dealing with these proprietary issues. In an intensely competitive market, the company secrets must be kept inviolate. However, after the staff meeting today, they heard some whispered speculations that someone has been leaking information to a major competitor.

Shanice and Clarence had both interviewed for a supervisory position; both were qualified. Shanice was offered the job and now supervises Clarence. She heard him complaining bitterly to a coworker about that decision, including some talk about "getting even." She fears Clarence may have breached his pledge to the company but has no proof. She is also afraid of what it may look like if she is the one to bring up any questions about Clarence.

■ What are the issues of covenant in this situation? Has a covenant been broken?

■ How might this situation escalate? How might it be defused?

■ What might you do in Shanice's place? in Clarence's?

■ What are the potential consequences of any proposed actions?

■ What scriptures or spiritual beliefs would inform your decision?

■ If a covenant has been broken, what might be done to restore it?

SERVICE LEARNING OPTIONS

Consider undertaking some of the projects mentioned below to enhance your study of the biblical idea of covenant. You may find them transformational as well as helpful!

IDEA #1: Become Good Stewards of the Planet

This project may be as simple as starting a recycling campaign at church, college, or the workplace; or advanced enough to bring together local construction and landscape architects to discuss how to make your town or city a sustainable, ecologically-friendly environment. Or host an Earth Day party at a local school or church, teaching others how we can take care of God's world on a daily basis through saving energy, recycling, and protecting farmland and forests.

IDEA #2: Covenant With Persons Living With AIDS

Ask your pastor about local organizations that provide assistance and aid to persons living with AIDS. Contact these organizations to find ways your study group could make a difference in a person's life on a regular basis. Something as simple as cooking a meal, cleaning a home, or running some errands could make a tremendous, positive impact one. Find out the potential consequences of taking on such a covenant for more than a short-term, "feel-good" time limit.

IDEA #3: Establish a VSSG

A Volunteer Services Singles Group is an organization of volunteers who share a common interest in helping those in need while volunteering alongside others who are single. The focus on VSSG is first on volunteering; meeting others and having social events would grow from the volunteering. A VSSG attracts people who want to do more volunteer work, or have already been volunteering and want to have the opportunity to meet other singles with similar interests. For more information on establishing a Single Volunteers Group, look up "Single Volunteers" on the World Wide Web.